THE RE SET

RETURNING TO
THE HEART OF
WORSHIP AND
A LIFE OF
UNDIVIDED
DEVOTION

JEREMY RIDDLE

THE RESET

RETURNING TO THE HEART OF WORSHIP
AND A LIFE OF UNDIVIDED DEVOTION

JEREMY RIDDLE

Published by Wholehearted Publishing
Anaheim, CA

Printed in the United State of America

ISBN 978-1-7362666-9-4

Interior Design by Josh Warner
Cover Design by Felix Eichhorn

The Reset is Book One in Whole-Heart-ed Series: Living and Leading a Life of Pure Worship

Author's website: www.JeremyRiddle.com

DEDICATIONS

To my children, Rebekah, Levi, Faith, Claire and Joseph. May each of you carry this charge forward and burn with love for the Lord. May you carry a greater zeal for the purity of worship than I ever did and champion His Name among the nations. I love you very much.

To my wife, Katie. Your love and friendship have purified, sharpened, refined and built me up into the man I am today. This book would not exist without you. I love you.

To my mom and dad, Edwin and Deborah. You have laid such a strong and beautiful foundation of purity and worship in my life. I'm so glad we got to labor over this work together and see it across the finish line. Thank you.

To my leaders and friends, Alan and Kathryn Scott. Your lives of holiness and wisdom have changed my life. This book would have been a far lesser and feebler work without your partnership and oversight. Thank you.

To my friends and co-laborers, Jen Miskov and Kieran De la Harpe. You were more than editors; you were shapers and contributors to this work. Deeply grateful for your labor of love! Thank you.

To my friends and Brazilian brothers, Cristiano Rede and Mateus Mainhard. Thank you for your every administrative, editing and recording effort on behalf of this book as well as your prophetic encouragement along the way. It is finally finished! Thank you.

CONTENTS

FOREWORD
BY ALAN SCOTT

What you have in your hands is more than a book, it's a manifesto; an urgent call for the resetting and restoration of worship in our time.

It has never been more necessary.

These are days where God grieves over the condition of His church. Celebration has replaced contrition; platforms have usurped altars, and greed has grown unconfronted. We are recognized by our ripped jeans instead of our torn hearts, our management rather than our covenants, our reputation on the earth rather than our contrition before heaven.

A long prophesied reformation is coming and must come. Wholehearted devotion will arise in the earth and along with it, the awareness that judgement lies over the nations. God will gain glory for His name. He will be exalted in all the earth.

This book is not for the fainthearted. It is sobering.

Jeremy writes like he worships; with skill and zeal, with honor and fire, intensity and humility. He is wholehearted and full-throated, challenging yet inviting. His pen serves as a healing sword as he cuts away impostors in our affections and rivals for God's glory. He articulately, incisively and passionately reminds us of the consecration that adds weight to our celebrations and the surrender that strengthens our songs. He writes with the insight, humility and passion of one who carries kingdom expectation at his core.

Although this is a book on reset, it is not the product of disillusionment or disappointment. This is holy anguish; it is crafted longing poured out onto pages. The lament that something precious and vital has been lost.

And it has.

We have traded secrecy for notoriety, our birthright for a brand. The sound of worship has replaced the wound of covenant. Our expressions are greater than our affections. We profess to give God our hearts, but what we give Him is our agendas. We are broken and bankrupt, yet too proud to admit our condition.

We have lost something vital, but we have not lost everything.

And that is the joy of *The Reset*. With hope, Jeremy summons us to reorder our souls, our services and our structures. He upsets some of our priorities and practices. He adds fuel to the disruption in calling for a worship reformation.

The resetting of worship overturns the current popular practices of worship. It offends the worship "industry" but delights those who value covenant above commerce. It throws out everything not aligned with the heart of the Father. It moves worship from focusing upon the horizontal to the vertical. Every platform to man removed. Every effort at popularity removed. Every idol of promotion removed. Using ministry to gain wealth removed. Using ministry to appear important removed. Using ministry to increase visibility removed. Every exploitation of people to fulfill our dreams removed. Every ignoring of the poor and seeking the friendship of the powerful removed. The cleansing of the temple has never been more necessary.

The idea that Jesus would be impressed by what we have built to make Him famous, or that He would leave our models of worship intact is vain. We are too timid to tear down the temple ourselves, too afraid to confront the excesses. We allow things to stand which, when moved by the Spirit, must be pulled down; edifices for our own importance, born from our ego rather than by His Spirit.

The cleansing of our modern temples has begun. It will continue with greater acceleration. God is raising up a new generation of worshippers who are more focused on building an altar than altering their world. They have promised their hearts to one love. They cannot and will not be turned. They are the relentless ones...who carry the soil of surrender. And this is their time.

I am thankful for Jeremy's conviction and his courage in leading the charge. This book is poignant and powerful, pastoral and prophetic. May it lead to unapologetic, unashamed, unadulterated worship in the earth. May the Lord use it to disturb those who have drifted, to re-ignite those whose hearts have grown cold, and to revive all who hunger and thirst.

Alan Scott,
Senior Pastor
Dwelling Place Anaheim

INTRODUCTION

I am writing this book to you as a man pierced. This is not the book I was inspired to write. This is the book *I had to write*. I am writing it in the middle of my own moment of "reset" and whole-hearted returning to the Lord.

The Lord commanded Isaiah to,

> **"Cry aloud; do not hold back; lift up your voice like a trumpet; declare to my people their transgression."**
> Isaiah 58:1

I know there are moments when it's important for leaders to con-strain their voices, but there are also moments when we *must not* hold back. For me, this book is the latter.

I don't believe there has been a moment in history when the temptation to be a worship leader for all the wrong reasons has ever been greater, never a moment where the seduction of per-sonal glory, fame, followers, adulation, money, self-gratification and earthly reward has more surrounded and infected this pre-cious thing we call worship. This has caused me so much grief and near despair just as it has tempted my own soul.

But this hope anchors me. There is also no greater time for *true, pure and undefiled worship* to rise on the earth than now. I can feel it growing in the hidden places. God is raising up those with clean hands and pure hearts. When the counterfeit is widely circulated, the genuine becomes that much more distinct, precious and powerful. That which is done from love and love alone, is pure. We will find all else was noise before His throne—all other motives and agendas found wanting before Him.

I wrote this book because I believe the worship movement and its leaders stand in the valley of decision, a decision we must make quickly and decisively. We are standing in the midst of one of the greatest worship awakenings in all history. But the question is, *how are we stewarding it*? How have we been responding to the mighty breath of God awakening His bride to worship in wonder again? *Are we squandering this moment?* Are we simply using it to build our professional songwriting and worship leading careers while platforming on our newfound "celebrity" status in a Christian bubble?

Let me ask, how many of us got into this to be professionals? Or to lead shallow nights of performance-based worship where we know the formula better than we know His Presence? Will any of us *come out of this*? And I literally mean *come out*! Abandon. Forsake. Be separate from. Will we cease playing Christian music games, blindly following current church trends, and writing songs for perceived needs and appetites in our Christian niche in hopes of striking gold with a hit radio single? Will we ever seek to reclaim that true prophetic edge in our songwriting and worship leading? Will we ever forsake our formulas and cry out for the true empowerment of the Holy Spirit on our lives again?

My friends, I too have been tempted, sifted, caught up in and blinded by many of these same pitfalls. I am not judging, I'm simply pleading that we recognize the sovereign hand of God moving in this hour, and with fear and trembling, *consecrate our lives afresh*—our gifts, platforms, and favor—to see an even greater awakening and release of His glory on the earth. Will we yield the whole of our lives again? Will we earnestly repent and return to the purity we started in? Will we forsake the earthly and foolish ambition that currently abounds and masquerades as spirituality? Will we respond to His moving by cleaning house and purging the inner chambers of our own temples from all that has corrupted and polluted first love?

I must make this appeal. We must re-adhere our lives and ministries to the standard of Scripture instead of the current "worship" culture that has made corruption common. If we choose to live by comparison to our current environment instead of the standard of Scripture—simply mimicking what has become common and acceptable practice amongst churches, worship departments, worship leaders, songwriters, musicians, and labels—we are in great danger of making a mockery and an idol out of the very thing meant to exalt Jesus. In so many ways, we already have. This should cause us no small amount of grief. As Matt Redman so poignantly wrote, "I'm sorry Lord for the thing I've made it (worship), when it's all about You. It's all about You Jesus."[1] If this was true over twenty years ago, how much truer is it today.

I feel an ever-growing burden and ache inside of me for this younger generation. When we're young, we first learn the danger of something from the emotional response of our parents or "elders" and that sharp, warning tone in their voice. Many of you have watched this play out. You're at a gathering where young families are milling about, and conversation is bubbling all around. Then a child, in complete innocence and curiosity, reaches towards a hot flame. All of a sudden, his parent's voice cracks like a whip over the noise, *"NO!! Don't touch!!"* The child immediately freezes in startled shock. Wide eyed fear overcomes his expression, and he may even burst into tears at the severity of the rebuke. The child may not fully understand his parent's intensity, *but he will never look at fire the same way again.* He's forever imprinted by the level of his parent's emotional response.

I know some of you may not understand my intensity at times in the following chapters, but I feel I must let it stand and imprint how it will. I would rather risk being misunderstood than remain silent as a ministry I so dearly love continues to be led down a destructive path.

In the medical field, what often appears to be a "harsh" treatment is only a physician applying the necessary force the healing of an injury requires. A broken bone that has never healed properly must be broken again in order to be reset. Otherwise, the person would remain permanently crippled. The same is true spiritually. There are more than a few broken bones deeply crippling the ministry of worship, and they must be reset. A bandage may appear to be the more merciful response, but bandages do not heal broken bones.

My deep longing is to see the tabernacle of worship restored and the heart of worship revived. I long to see the worshiping church not only led into repentance and reform, *but on into glory.* This is where she was made to live; where she becomes beautiful and radiant. This is where she flourishes and produces every good work. It is in the glory she begins to look like Him, think like Him, and act like Him.

My greatest desire for you as you read this book is that Jesus would become your one and all-consuming desire. I pray that if there's anything competing or taking the edge off of your desire for Him or if there's any place in your heart where other things are starting to seduce and "dazzle" you more, that reading this book would be a moment of divine reset in your heart. I pray this journey will be the beginning of a new chapter in your life marked by greater purity and power.

RECLAIMING WORSHIP

CHAPTER 1

Wherever God is worshiped in spirit and in truth, His kingdom is established, His freedom reigns, and the works of the devil are destroyed. Pure praise has always been a weapon of mass destruction to the kingdom of darkness. This is why Satan, the sworn enemy of God, hates the song of the redeemed and the praises of the Lamb more than any other sound on earth. Because he is a killer, a stealer, and a destroyer, he has been hell-bent on destroying the worship movement long before it ever had a chance at maturity. He was aware of its great, destructive power to his realm of darkness long before we were. We just thought we were singing simple love songs to Jesus and were almost oblivious to the fact we were simultaneously destroying the gates of hell.

But our enemy was patient. He was crafty. And at present, he is wildly succeeding in his mission to destroy the purity of worship. Worse, we are allowing him. At times even partnering with him. Every time we allow idolatry, humanism, pride, falseness, heresy, celebrity, self-indulgence, debauchery, sensuality, and so many other forms of worldliness and wickedness to parade around, uninhibited in our houses of worship, *we partner with his destructive work*. The worship movement may look better and sound better than it ever did in the past, but as a whole, it is but a shadow of its former purity, power and anointing. The sound is huge. The personalities are large. The stages are bright. The crowds are enthused.

But so often, all I can hear is noise. All I can feel is grief.

Grief over my own unawareness.

Grief over all the times I contributed to the noise.

Grief over any part I ever played in bringing us to this point.

Grief over any time I kept my mouth shut in the name of keeping the peace.

Grief over every time I felt a check in my spirit but ignored it and just went along with the crowd.

In my grief, I find my heart crying out, "Oh where is the sound of purity in worship? Where is the sound of hearts free of self-indulgent agendas and utterly enraptured by Him? Where is that sweet, thick anointing? Oh where, oh where are You Holy Spirit and where is Your precious presence? Where has it gone? Where did we lose it? HOW did we get here?"

But most importantly I find myself asking...

"Can we get it back?"

And this is the question: Is it possible reclaim the purity of this beautiful gift we call worship? Is it possible to snatch it back from the hands of its destroyer, and to see it restored not simply to its former glory, but to a far greater glory than we have EVER seen manifest on the earth? To the realness and trueness of *His glory*?

I would not be writing this if I believed we couldn't.

A BIT OF WORSHIP HISTORY

We live in a day of fulfilled dreams. Over the last sixty years we have seen the worship movement expand and grow in remarkable and unprecedented ways. Currently, there are more worship songs being written, more worship projects being released, more worship bands playing, and more worship leaders leading than at any other time in history. The generation before us *dreamed of this day*. They dreamed of a great revival of worship in the church. Their church landscape looked nothing like ours. Worship was all but dead; shrouded in religion and empty form. Greatly lacking heart, vibrancy and freedom. The prophet A.W. Tozer said, "Worship was the missing jewel in modern evangelicalism."² And it was true.

The previous generation began to dream of a day when worship would once again regain a place of centrality in the church. They prayed, contended, and labored towards that end. Oh, the roadblocks and opposition! Oh, the price pioneers must pay! And we think we're persecuted now? They are the ones who had to painstakingly disassociate the style of rock-n-roll music from the "realm of the devil." Back then everyone knew that rock-n-roll was the "devil's music." It was nearly impossible for them to see electric bass, guitars, and drums as anything other than "satanic." The acoustic guitar might have been a shoo-in but to disassociate the "demonic realm" from the electric guitar was an entirely different matter. We will probably never know what it cost them to perform this slow, arduous surgery. I say all this with a bit of tongue in cheek, but these were *real* struggles they faced.

We haven't even touched on clothing styles and men with long hair. That was a whole other realm of warfare. Truly, we just have to marvel. Now, an electric guitarist can just waltz onto a church stage with his snakeskin boots, tats, rings, necklaces, looking like he just played a Rolling Stones show and...*no one blinks an eye*. This is amazing. The generation before us could scarce believe a day of freedom like this would actually come! And we owe them. They were the ones who fought and bled to take the territory we now get to experience as our everyday reality. They literally *fought* for our freedom.

The funny thing about freedom is, it's way trickier to navigate than a legalistic system of clear do's and don'ts. It's one thing to navigate a narrow path with strict guard rails; it's quite another to navigate a vast, open expanse of uncharted wilderness. I for one am so grateful for the freedom we have today, and I *never* want to pendulum swing back into past legalism.

But there is something we must understand.

The generation before us did not fight the good fight for freedom so we could all become worship celebrities, write hit songs, tour the globe and live like the rich and famous. NO. I am positive this is not the expression they had in mind.

They fought for that freedom, so we could break the bottle... So that we could *freely* pour out the fragrance of our love and adoration on Jesus and do it through all the musical, physical, emotional, and artistic ways our hearts burned to do so. Unashamed and unhindered.

And this is the thing we must reclaim. I believe the generation before us knew what was at stake. They weren't simply fighting for the freedom of their own artistic expression; they were fighting for a generation yet to come. If they had chosen to leave worship steeped and bound in religion and had not fought that battle for us, a whole generation of leaders would have never emerged. Their purpose and assignment would have been stillborn. I believe I would have been one of those stillborn leaders; most likely trying to build a successful law practice somewhere in New Jersey and utterly unaware of what was on my life for worship. If it hadn't been for pioneers like Randy Stonehill, Larry Norman, Keith Green, my parents and later on worship forerunners like Kevin Prosch and Delirious, that part of my heart and calling would have never woken up.

My friends, the same is true for us. As my friend Ray Hughes once said, "You're not a part of a five-year plan, you're a part of a generational one." It is our turn to fight the good fight of faith. There is a war raging right now over this next generation, and we get to determine whether they "wake up" to their calling and destiny because of the blazing brightness of our passion for Jesus, or whether they drift away into other pursuits because of our compromise and earthly ambitions. If we persist on our current path, not only will we squander the previous ground of freedom our mothers and fathers fought to gain for us, we will silence a whole generation of worshipers our lives were intended to awaken.

THE DESIGN OF THE DEVIL

One of the worst things we can do is to glorify the power of Satan. But the second worst thing we can do is to be ignorant of him. Paul highlighted this in 2 Corinthians 2:11 when he mentioned, *"that we would not be outwitted by Satan, for we are not ignorant of his designs."* When we remain ignorant of the devil's designs, we are easily outwitted by him.

Here is the truth: we live in a spiritual war zone. You may not like this truth, but it is truth all the same. In a war zone there is no neutral ground. Something or someone is always trying to take you out, rob you of your legacy, your destiny, your faith and your purity. We cannot afford to be ignorant of the ministry graveyards we walk through; the war ground littered with bodies, unmarked graves and names the world has long forgotten because their destinies were cut short. We live in a spiritual battle and though we don't wage it against flesh and blood, the casualties are still real. Some of them have been my friends.

Do you know you were made to carry glory? Eternal, holy, glory? Paul tells us in 2 Corinthians 4:17, we are being prepared for an *"eternal weight of glory beyond all comparison."* Even now, we've been invited by the Father of all glory, to be sons and daughters *filled with His glory* and radiating His divine presence. There have been many times leading worship where I have felt His glory come on me. And there were these other times when His glory just stayed on me, long after the set was through, resting on me like an ever-present invitation to live in that place. To even remember these times floods me with an anguished longing for more of Him. There is simply *nothing* like it.

But the enemy is trying to seduce a whole generation into the pursuit of its counterfeit: *to become a celebrity instead of a person who carries glory.* Darker still, he is seducing a generation into *capitalizing* on the glory of God as a means to that end.

The enemy loves counterfeiting the real thing. He loves seducing people into partnering with his demoralizing works through the clever peddling of partial truths. And how easily we keep being seduced! The idol of influence is wreaking havoc in the church in our time, and we, like the world, are in hot pursuit of it. In the world and in the church, Instagram accounts of hundreds of thousands of followers are beginning to act like a form of modern-day currency. But hear me when I say this: an Instagram account of millions of followers is nothing but a cheap bowl of soup in comparison to the *birthright of heaven's glory resting upon your life*. Don't be a fool and trade one to get the other!

The seduction of influence is not the only tactic of the enemy. With the ones he can't lead into the pursuit of celebrity he leads into disillusionment, disappointment, offense and ultimately *disengagement*. Many have already checked out or have been taken out. I have known precious people who carried such tremendous anointing in the area of worship but who took themselves out of action simply because they couldn't overcome the wounding, the rejection, or stomach the political games churches play. My heart is still broken over these ones.

But I remain a prisoner of hope. I believe this can change. I believe *WE* can change it. More than that, I believe we *must* change it. We cannot afford to shrink back, and we cannot fail. There is too much at stake.

We *must* dethrone entertainment in the church. We *must* dethrone the spirit of performance that is born of the flesh. We *must* dethrone the lust for influence and fame in leadership. We *must* dethrone the western world's "worship celebrity culture" we have freely shared with the nations and caused them to stumble into the same idolatry!! *Woe to us*! We *must* dethrone selfish ambition. It must get out of our hearts and off our stages and podiums. To even allow it on the smallest scale is ruinous. James 3:16 lays out the costly consequence and states:

> **Where jealousy and selfish ambition exist,**
> **there will be disorder and every vile practice.**

It is my burning mission to see purity in worship restored to the house of God. I'm determined to see whatever obstacles that oppose true worship removed and torn down. I'm determined to see an uncompromising generation rise and flood the earth with the mighty sound of His glory! For too long have I watched an industry, well-intentioned or not, steer the decisions, motivations, tone, sound, and language of worship. For too long have I watched so many precious, anointed worship leaders become corrupted by the pressures and temptations that surround them.

Worship is not an industry. It's not a platform. It's not about worship leaders, worship projects, new songs, new artists, new movements, or new brands. Worship is *not a trade*. It is not a career path or a professional line of work we get to do. Worship is the sound of a *covenantal people*; a people betrothed to Jesus. It is the sound of their love, adoration, and zealous devotion to the only One found worthy!

I don't have much faith in mass social media campaigns or other large-scale attempts to effect change. Some have worked. Most haven't. But I do believe in the power of the Holy Spirit moving through the radical commitment of a few. Not only do I believe God can take a few and turn the tide for the masses, *I have personally seen it*. It's also all throughout Scripture. One of my favorite Old Testament stories is the story of Jonathan and his armor bearer going up against a whole army of their enemy, the Philistines. Jonathan's words of faith in 1 Samuel 14:6 ring in my ears,

> *It may be that the Lord will work for us, for nothing can hinder the Lord from saving by many or by FEW.*

I am writing this to invite those few into a journey of radical obedience and surrender. I'm urging you to do anything and everything in your power to set things right. I charge you to reform and revive the heart of worship within the church and to do it with your life, love, purity and zeal. You have no idea how powerful your one little life can be. You have no idea how powerful your small little church community can be. What is impossible for man, is not impossible for God.

I believe that if a *few* repent for what we've made this thing called worship...

That if a *few* begin to move in the spirit of Josiah, whose zeal reformed and purified the worship of his entire nation...

If a *few* refuse to compromise...

Then a *few*...can reset this thing.

And with God's hand upon us, we will.

THE POWER OF PURITY

CHAPTER 2

I have long understood the power of purity. Something can only be as powerful as it is pure. Some would argue that love is the greatest power, but even love will only be as powerful as it is pure. Purity may not be the flashiest thing or the coolest, but when purity comes onto the scene, it arrests the room. It strikes the deepest chord. Purity has such a mystifying power to it. If you think about it, purity isn't powerful because its overbearing or because it's forceful. In fact, there is no striving in it. It's powerful simply because *it is*.

A lot of times, we don't know how dirty something is until purity comes on the scene. You can think of yourself as a generally clean person, but if you wear a white shirt for a day, chances are your thinking will change. It's not that your white shirt is being vindictive, it's just revealing how clean you really are. Purity has a way of exposing all lesser things. It reveals all things cheapened, polluted and compromised. Again, it's not that purity is trying to make anything and anyone else look bad, it just has an *exposing power*. When present, it effortlessly reveals the truth and the actual reality in any situation.

The same is true in the context of worship. Pure worship will always be the most powerful kind and expose all lesser offerings.

But what do you do when purity is lost? How do you return to it again? The path is not easy. To recover something's original vibrancy and power, you often have to reduce it back to its raw, organic beginnings. In our case, this would be worship before stages, bands, industry, crowds, production, social media, albums, schools, programs and all the modern-day church agendas and logistics we are now forced to navigate. One of the most beautiful things you will discover in this reduction process is that the power of worship isn't connected to any of the trappings we surround it with, and it doesn't stem from any of the things we typically add to it.

For instance, you can take a worshiping people...add a person with an acoustic guitar, add a band, stage, lights, screens, powerful mountain imagery, lots of fog, and wrap the best sonic experience money can buy around it...and you will certainly make it louder and more visually stimulating, *but you won't make it more powerful.*

The reason is simple: *the heart of worship has nothing to do with any of these things.* Worship will never get more powerful the more things you add to it because its power has never flowed from its form. *Its power has always flowed from His presence.* But you will not discover any significant measure of His presence without purity and holiness. The farther you get away from purity, the hollower and more lifeless everything begins to sound.

Many things *start pure,* but few things *end pure.* It's sobering to think of how many people and movements started in purity, but how few of those same people and movements ended there.

PURITY AND POPULARITY

I want to be very clear that I'm not anti-influence or popularity if it is the result of the Lord's favor. But regardless, I do know first-hand that popularity will sift you like nothing else. If idleness is the devil's workshop, then popularity is his playground. It's still the fastest way to kill the purity of something I know of. Just make it *popular.*

So, this begs the question: Is it possible to be popular and pure? Can one survive it and still remain true to God? The answer is, yes. *But only if purity has a knife to popularity's throat, ready to annihilate it the moment a conflict arises.* This kind of intensity is crucial. And I'm not just talking about the big conflicts and compromises. I'm talking about the *slightest ones.* You will never win your bigger battles if you aren't diligent with the smaller ones.

But we have One who has gone before us and given us a clear path.

Jesus was incredibly popular, but He was never *led* by His popularity. He only allowed Himself to be led by His Father. He was obedient to His Father on the days when thousands gathered to Him and obedient on the days when thousands left Him. It's so easy for us to start in purity, gain popularity, and subtly begin to serve our "followers" instead of the Lord. But if Jesus never allowed popularity to guide His choices or His teachings, then neither can we.

I will also suggest that our enemy isn't nearly as concerned about our popularity as he is our level of purity. I don't think he looks at anyone's celebrity status on social media and "shudders" with fear. If anything, it's probably the opposite. But I do believe he greatly fears undivided devotion and purity of heart.

THE WELLSPRING OF LIFE

When you protect the purity of something, the essence of its original purpose and design, you guard its *heart*. By doing this, you preserve its life. The famous verse in Proverbs 4:23 says it best:

> *Keep your heart with all vigilance,*
> *for from it flow the springs of life.*

A well-guarded heart is the key to life.

This same principle applies to the heart of worship. If we fail to guard the heart of worship with *all vigilance,* it will cease to carry the life and revival it was meant to bring to our hearts and to the earth. Indeed, it appears we are already failing in this regard. Our worship events might be selling out, but our culture is in rapid moral decline, as are many attending and leading these same worship events. This indicates something is quite amiss. Our volume may be increasing, but the heartbeat of true worship is growing faint.

So how do we guard the heart of worship with all vigilance? How do we preserve its life? It is fairly simple. *We never let worship become about anything other than Jesus.* Loving Jesus. Glorifying Jesus. *Exalting, honoring, and ministering to Jesus.* Currently, one of the greatest dangers to the purity of worship is the worship of worship itself and those who lead it. This is not a new danger. The most sobering thought any worship leader could ever have is that the arch nemesis of God might have been one of us before he fell.

When we allow worship to become about a worship leader, a song, a musical expression, a church growth agenda, a brand, an industry, a musical gig, a personal need for breakthrough, or any other agenda that is self-seeking and self-serving—*anything besides ministering to Jesus*—we allow the life it carries to be trampled out of it.

A PICTURE OF PURITY

They say a picture is worth a thousand words and there is truth to that. Sometimes all we need is a picture of what pure worship looks like to remember again. Not everything can be described, some things must be witnessed. The Gospel of Luke gives us such a picture when it describes a prostitute who publicly and extravagantly ministered to Jesus at a dinner party in a Pharisee's house.

> *One of the Pharisees asked him to eat with him, and he went into the Pharisee's house and reclined at table. And behold, a woman of the city, who was a sinner, when she learned that he was reclining at table in the Pharisee's house, brought an alabaster flask of ointment, and standing behind him at his feet, weeping, she began to wet his feet with her tears and wiped them with the hair of her head and kissed his feet and anointed them with the ointment.* Luke 7:36-38

The language surrounding this encounter has become so used and the story so frequently told, I fear its impact is lost on us. It's difficult to convey the magnitude of this moment or the sheer shockingness of this exchange. *It was a scene!* It deeply troubled everyone who witnessed it. But this exchange between Jesus and this woman has so much to teach us about what deeply moves the heart of God.

I want to focus on three key things this moment reveals about purity in worship. I know if these three things were to be re-embodied in a generation, they would turn the world upside down.

1. Pure Worship is Costly

Traditionally, there has been so much emphasis on how costly the alabaster flask of ointment was that this woman broke at the feet of Jesus. Some speculate it was worth a year of wages. But this wasn't just a costly jar of perfume she was breaking at the feet of Jesus. It was a costly act for anyone who wished to retain an ounce of dignity and self-respect within his or her social context.

Out of all the things humans guard most fiercely, self-image might win the day. But this woman completely disregarded hers. I imagine her heart was beating out of her chest. I'm sure she couldn't have been ignorant as to how people would "interpret" her actions or how harshly she was about to be judged. But she just couldn't stop herself. She broke not only a bottle of expensive perfume at His feet, she broke all her personal dignity and self-respect with it.

We have to remember, *no one else got it.* Not one person in the group of onlookers was analyzing the situation and thinking, "Ya know, this is going to inspire a lot of beautiful worship songs down the road." No one wrote on social media that night, "Wow...I just witnessed one of the most beautiful acts of worship." There was no riveting photo. No glowing quote. In fact, quite the opposite. There was only outrage and judgment.

No one thought that was the right thing to do in the moment.

I repeat. *No one.*

No one...*but Jesus. Jesus did.* Jesus was moved by it. Jesus knew what it cost her. Jesus knew the purity of it. And He made this decree:

> **Truly, I say to you, wherever this gospel is proclaimed in the whole world, what she has done will also be told in memory of her.** Matthew 26:13

Pause for a moment.

Can you imagine *how shocking* this must have been for the people around him to hear? They were probably thinking, "Jesus, *that*!? That awkward moment where none of us knew what to do? That moment where we all felt we should probably rescue you or at least felt you should probably rescue yourself? That moment? *That moment gets eternally linked with the proclamation of the gospel*?!"

Yes. *That moment.*

We must grasp this: p*ure worship has nothing to gain in the realm of popularity.* It could care less. It *only* hopes to touch the heart; to win the heart of the One it is worshiping. It is *never* driven by the benefit it gets. It is so blinded by the depth of its love it cannot possibly adhere to what the social norms of the day deem to be "acceptable." Pure worship is solely driven by the "*I HAVE TO LET YOU KNOW...I have to communicate to You somehow, someway...how much You mean to me...how much*

You've touched my life..." It's extreme. It will go to any length and pay any cost to demonstrate the depth of its love and gratitude.

Know this. The next time you witness a scene where the whole room is made uncomfortable and offended by someone's over the top response in worship, there's a real good chance God felt *loved by it.*

Let me ask, how many things do we do in worship that cost us nothing? How many things don't we do because it *will* cost us something? Worship without cost is worship without impact. King David declared in 2 Samuel 24:24, "*I will not offer burnt offerings to the Lord my God that cost me nothing.*" When we begin to step beyond our comfort zones, beyond how emotional we're feeling in the moment, beyond whatever has become our "customary" and normal response in worship and *begin to give Him that which costs us something...*we will begin to discover purity in worship. To offer God our dignity, our self-respect, our personal, emotional, and financial comfort, is to offer Him something costly. This is pleasing to His heart.

2. Pure Worship is Eternal

Pure worship, that sweet, "heart-begotten" praise, expressed solely through faith and love, is the only kind of worship that will leave a lasting impact on the earth, on eternity and on the heart of God. If you're doing what you're doing for notoriety, influence, and significance in the eyes of men, not only will your reward fade along with this earth, you will *never* touch the heart of God.

And there is no fooling God.

He is the only one who knows the purity of our offerings. We're not even qualified to judge ourselves most days. I have often been sobered when reading 1 Corinthians 3:12-15 where Paul states:

Now if anyone builds on the foundation with gold, silver, precious stones, wood, hay, straw— each one's work will become manifest, for the Day will disclose it, because it will be revealed by fire, and the fire will test what sort of work each one has done. If the work that anyone has built on the foundation survives, he will receive a reward. If anyone's work is burned up, he will suffer loss, though he himself will be saved, but only as through fire.

At the end of my life, I don't want to watch all of my worship offerings consumed by the fire because they were merely hay and stubble. Done for others. Impressive to the masses. But failing to touch the heart of the One who mattered most. I want my life to count for eternity. I don't want to be robbed of my eternal reward because I got caught in some kind of influence game down here. What a tragedy that would be!

Remember, *we get to choose our building materials*. We get to choose if it's going to be gold, silver, precious stones, or wood, hay, and stubble. If you've been building with the wrong material, you can change that. Starting today.

3. Pure Worship is Driven by Love

The future of worship does not belong to the most brilliant song writers, musical virtuosos, or gifted vocalists. *It belongs to lovers.* Those who will love their God with all their heart, soul, mind and strength. It was the woman who "*loved much*" who set the bar for worship. "Little love" will always produce "little worship." Love is the reset we need and the reformation we crave.

Love is a power greater than any other power. A person filled with love can overcome anything, accomplish anything. Love is the greatest force on earth, and we know the true source of it. *God is love*. Love is how He forever shamed and defeated the principalities and authorities of this world through the cross.

We are far too prone to underestimate the power and potency of love. Love is the only thing strong enough to lift the seduction of influence and the brokenness of selfish ambition off of our lives. Love is the only thing powerful enough to set us free from comparison, self-importance, self-obsession, pride, anxiety, insecurity and fear. Love literally expels those things from our hearts. Love is the only force capable of awakening this next generation of worshipers. It will not be all the newest and coolest things we keep chasing...it will only be the sound of pure love for Jesus.

Worship will be reclaimed by lovers.

A FIRM FOUNDATION

If you feel broken, unworthy, and inadequate as a worshiper or leader, God wants to reset you. He wants to give you a new foundation. One that is not built on your gifting, your charisma, or a long list of successful sets. He wants to show you the simplicity and power of love for Him. It is more than enough to change the world.

I so love all of the stories of Peter. He gives me so much hope! Peter relied on his passion, his strength and his boldness. One time he even tried to counsel the Lord as if he had a clearer understanding, which indicates a bit of pride. Peter was the one who declared Jesus to be the Christ and swore to die for the Lord. When Jesus was arrested, it was Peter who cut off the ear of the high priest's servant.

But Satan had asked to sift him like wheat. And Peter was sifted.

His strength failed. His zeal failed. In a moment, he denied everything he believed in. And the Lord looked right at him right after he did it.

You have to know Peter wanted a different story. I'm sure that's not how he wanted to be remembered. He wanted to stand head and shoulders above his brothers. He wanted to be the guy who emerged from that sifting steadfast. But the greatest gift from that sifting was in his restoration. Jesus asked Peter a simple question three times in John 21:15-17: *"Simon, Son of John, do you love me?"* And what else could Peter's broken heart reply? *"Yes, Lord, you know that I love you."*

At that moment, there was no pride. No zeal. No praise-worthy performance. No victorious overcoming story of faithfulness in the middle of testing. No demonstration of steadfastness above all his brothers. In fact, he was the only one to deny Jesus.

All Peter had left was love, his sincere love for Jesus. And from that day on, love became his new foundation.

When life sifts you, when disappointment and offense come at you, when pain shakes you, when failure threatens to overwhelm you...*let it reduce you to love*. Love is the only foundation God desires to build upon.

Forget there is an industry. Forget there is a career to be had or a model of how to be a "worship leader." That model is broken. Instead, *be someone in love.*

Love is the *only qualifier* in worship.

Love is the only thing that really carries that anointing.

Love is the only authority you have.

Love is the only difference between a song and a ringing gong.

Love is the only thing that determines whether your life and your sound will have meaning, longevity, and purpose in the earth and in heaven.

Your job is to love Jesus well. Not "kill" the worship leader game. Often times when I hear worship leaders lead, love is not the thing I experience. So many other new agendas have crept in. New vocal styles. New worship moves. New facial expressions. Fresh song choices and so much "coolness." Sometimes I just want to sweep the table clear and say, *"Just show me your love for Jesus!"*

Love leads me in.

Love opens my heart.

Love renews my passion.

Lead me in *LOVE...*

Only the pure fire of your love for Jesus can ignite the church and the world in worship. A nice Christian performance will never carry this fire.

But a people who break their alabaster jar...A people who risk everything to fall at the feet of Jesus and say "I love You" with their tears, their kisses, and their extravagant ministry to Him...

Will.

So, let the fire of love be the most visible thing on your life.

Let your power flow from your purity, not your performance.

Let your power flow from the genuineness of your love for Jesus and the sincerity of your heart for Him.

Anchor yourself to this firm and lasting foundation. Be rooted In love.

THE FOUR MARKS OF A WORSHIP REFORMER

CHAPTER 3

I have long been gripped with the story of Jesus cleansing the temple. This is the only occasion recorded in Scripture where Jesus used physical force against anything or anyone. If there was a prize for the most "frequently taken out of context" scripture, this would certainly be a strong contender. It has been wrongfully used to justify all kinds of self-righteous and angry nonsense. But this passage isn't about a lack of anger management, this passage is about the state of worship, prayer, and conduct in the house of God. This is about a moment of divine visitation and holy correction. The Son of God visited His Father's house and with an all-consuming zeal, drove out all that disgraced and dishonored it. There is a holy reformation in this text.

Scripture records this story in the Gospel of John:

> *The Passover of the Jews was at hand, and Jesus went up to Jerusalem. In the temple he found those who were selling oxen and sheep and pigeons, and the money-changers sitting there. And making a whip of cords, he drove them all out of the temple, with the sheep and oxen. And he poured out the coins of the money-changers and overturned their tables.*

And he told those who sold the pigeons, "Take these things away; do not make my Father's house a house of trade." John 2:13-16

The Gospel of Mark also records this:

And he was teaching them and saying to them, "Is it not written, 'My house shall be called a house of prayer for all the nations.'" Mark 11:17

Use your imagination for a moment. Play this out in your mind. Jesus, our Lord and King, walks into the temple and actually takes the time *to make a whip.* Then He descends in a bewildering fury on unsuspecting money changers and merchandisers, flinging his whip, kicking over tables, and scattering money, livestock, and merchandise.

It is important we don't glance over this too quickly or dismiss its intensity. *This was no light correction.* Clearly, there was a significant violation at play and one that provoked an all out upheaval from Jesus. This moment might have happened 2000 years ago, but lest we forget, Jesus is no less *consumed with zeal over His spiritual house today.* We would be wise to ask ourselves if there are things taking place in the area of modern worship that would provoke the same level of response and righteous indignation from Him.

THE JESUS MODEL

One quick glance through church history should tell us that whenever Jesus ceases to be exalted as the model for our lives and ministries, things immediately get weird. And dark. But this is a mistake we keep on repeating. One of the biggest issues at work in the church today is its *constant mimicking of itself.* Not Scripture. Not the model of Jesus. *But its own subculture.* Particularly now in the age of social media, it is the well-known worship leaders, pastors and church movements who have inadvertently become the new model—the image of success everyone is trying to duplicate and pattern.

But this current model of "worship celebrity" is *not* the model I want to see passed on to the next generation. This model is woefully lacking in the fire and purity of love; greatly wanting in the area of humility, holiness, reverence, and godliness. In fact, a quick scroll through social media reveals this model to be *full* of itself. Full of its own vanity, pride, and praise. This model looks nothing like Jesus, and I repent for any part that I've played in it. Even now the hint of it repulses and grieves me.

Oh, how we need the model of Jesus to be exalted again in our day! *I can hear the earth groaning for something that looks like Jesus.* Longing for a pure manifestation of the sons and daughters of God in our time! The ones who will shine His light and radiance into the darkness around them. The ones who will look like the One who didn't count equality with God something to be grasped, who didn't have a shred of pride or entitlement in His body or spirit, the One who forsook His throne, His glory, His wealth and His privilege to become poor, the One who came not to be served but to serve and to lay His life down, the One who demonstrated reverence, humility and obedience towards His Father, even unto a horrific death on a cross.

Oh, the glory of Jesus! The magnificence of Jesus!

Why would we seek to imitate anything or anyone else? Jesus is the only way, truth and light in a world gone mad with depravity.

I am longing for a true Jesus generation of worshipers and leaders to arise—*the ones who will have no other model but Him.* The worshipers and leaders who will take a stand in previous areas of compromise and have nothing to do with the broken and corrupted models handed down to them by their mothers and fathers. The ones who will be filled with the zeal of the Lord and committed to reforming and re-establishing His house *as a house of prayer for all nations.*

THE FOUR MARKINGS

I believe there are four distinct markings on Jesus' life that were visible at that moment of cleansing. These are desperately needed to reform and purify the realm of worship today. I've already begun to see these marks manifest on a rising generation and I believe many will follow. It is a work of the Spirit and will rest upon those in step with the Spirit.

1. They will have the eyes and ears of the Lord

The first mark on these reformers is discernment; a people who will be able to see and hear just as clearly as Jesus did. Scripture does not give us the impression anyone else was deeply disturbed by what was going on in the temple that day. No one else seemed to be raising a fuss or suspicious of its day to day activities. No one else seemed to be harassing the pigeon sellers or the merchandisers who were turning a profit off people coming to worship God. To everyone else, this was just another normal day of decades old temple practices that everyone seemed to have accepted.

Everyone, *but Jesus.*

Jesus had different eyes. Clear eyes. Bright eyes. Heaven's eyes. Eyes that could clearly see the corrupted, dishonorable, and greed-filled practices infesting His house.

Do you ever wonder why no one else saw this or addressed it? Or why Jesus' reaction was such a shock to all those around him? This is what happens when heaven's perspective is lost over time. Rome wasn't built in a day nor is a house of worship corrupted in one. It can take decades of slow, subtle compromise. Worldly culture is always trying to infect a heavenly one. If we're not constantly vigilant, we become like the frog in a slowly boiling pot of water, unable to discern the danger we are in until it's too late.

If you have ever spent time reading through the prophets, you will notice how God would go through great lengths to reach His people. At times, even communicating through "extreme" and bizarre pictures, sexual imagery, and language. For Instance, God commanded the prophet Hosea to marry a whore, someone who would frequently betray and cheat on him: *"for the land commits great whoredom by forsaking the Lord."*

When you read these prophetic letters to Israel you can literally feel God's desperation and longing to get through to them—ever trying to communicate the intensity of the pain their actions and betrayal were inflicting on His heart. He was always trying to get them to see: *"My covenant people!! When you do these things, this is how it makes Me feel!!"* Sadly, the people of Israel were frequently unable to see what the "big deal" was.

We are not so different. We have also lacked the eyes or the will to see as He sees.

Many times, I have sensed a strange, inappropriate relationship beginning to form between worship leaders and the people they're leading. I've observed when people become increasingly pulled into the tractor beam of someone's personal charisma, and when that leader begins to *feed on that* (I believe mostly unknowingly), they begin to lead people into intimacy with "themselves" instead of intimacy with Him. The more the celebrity worship leader model grows, the more common this becomes.

Leaders, we cannot allow this to continue. To even remotely interfere with the intimacy between the bride and the Groom in the place of worship is to violate our holy, priestly assignment *in every way*. This not only endangers us, but also endangers the ones we lead. If you sense this beginning to happen and people becoming increasingly focused on you during a worship time, quickly move people's attention back on Jesus. Begin to shift the room back into high praise. *Exhort the people to glorify the Lord!* Break with this model of celebrity and artist driven worship events because it is only causing this perversion to increase.

Please hear my heart on this. I'm not trying to get weird or condemn anyone. I understand the complexity of this issue as I have lived in it for more than a decade. I'm aware of how little control we have over what goes on in people's hearts while we're leading. I haven't always known what to do or had the wisdom or clarity to understand why things felt so "off" during certain times of worship or how to correct it. This has been a journey. But I do know the purity of a worship leader's heart can be felt in a room far more than we're aware of and that purity always determines whether the majority connect with Jesus, or with someone or something else.

The more I lean into the heartbeat of heaven, the more I begin to see the real "madness" of so much of our worship culture right now. We need eyes to see, just as Jesus did, the things that have become so routine, common, and normal in worship ministry, *but are so grievous to the heart of God.* We need eyes to see the things taking place on our stages, in our green rooms, in our worship communities, and on our "worship" tours and events that should not even be *named among us.*

Oh, how we need Spirit empowered eyes to see! We need discernment, wisdom, and revelation. We need to ask our Father for these things. We need to begin to pray bold prayers:

> *Heavenly Father give us the Spirit of wisdom and revela- tion in the knowledge of You. Take the blinders off of our eyes! Give us eyes to see how You see. Give us ears to hear what the Spirit is speaking to us. If we can't hear, we are truly lost without Helper or Guide. Give us hearing ears. Give us salve to anoint our eyes, so we can see. We want to be the ones who carry Your eyes, ears, and heart wherever we go.*

2. They will carry the zeal of the Lord for the house of the Lord

The second mark on these rising reformers is a tremendous zeal for the Lord and a zeal for His house. Zealous leaders are courageous leaders and much courage will be needed. The verse the disciples remembered in the middle of that holy, purging, pandemonium was Psalm 69:9, *"Zeal for your house has consumed me."* I imagine this wasn't too difficult to remember while plastered up against some temple wall watching Jesus *"teach."*

I have found zeal to be one of the most misunderstood things. Today, if you went around proclaiming to be *"consumed with zeal for the house of the Lord!"* you would probably risk being institutionalized. I have noticed that when anyone starts getting *zealous*, people start getting *nervous*. If you start talking, acting, and living "radically" for God (a.k.a. just doing what Jesus commanded), it's amazing how many people immediately seek to caution and temper you. Funny though, no one seems to warn you about the cost of living apathetically or in half-hearted obedience to His commands—this is *unspeakably more costly*.

But in spite of the confusion and misunderstanding, zeal is *vital* to the believer, and even more so to the *leading believer*. I love the Scripture in Isaiah 59:17 where it says God *"wrapped himself in zeal as a cloak."* What a picture! Zeal operates like a holy protection when we wrap ourselves in it. I have found I am at my best as a worshiper, leader, husband, father and friend, *when I am wrapped in zeal of the Lord*. It is only when I am lacking in zeal that I am most prone to compromise. This is why Paul instructs us in Romans 12:11, *"Do not be slothful in zeal, be fervent in spirit, serve the Lord."*

Worship leaders, always remember there is great warfare over your zeal. If you don't intentionally burn with zeal for the Lord, you will begin to burn with a zeal for something else. There really is no middle ground. The ploy of the enemy is to divide and re-direct your attention, your affections, and your desires. If you are trying to maintain zeal for your worship leading career and zeal for the house of the Lord, one will win. Probably your career. Again, we have made it so easy to spiritualize our own personal pursuit of glory and status. But our assignment was never to seek first the "kingdom of influence." It was always to seek first the kingdom of God.

Joshua made the people of Israel choose their allegiance as they entered the promised land saying,

> *And if it is evil in your eyes to serve the Lord, choose this day whom you will serve, whether the gods your fathers served in the region beyond the River, or the gods of the Amorites in whose land you dwell. But as for me and my house, we will serve the Lord.* Joshua 24:15

The same choice stands before you today. You must set your course now before the testing comes. It will surely come. There is always great testing in your promised land. You must make the choice now what zeal will consume you and keep you in consistent faithfulness to the Lord.

Do this moment justice. It may be the most important moment of your life. Build an altar of consecration you can return to again and again.

Ask yourself: What will I choose to be zealous for? What will I choose to be consumed by? What will I choose as the foundation of my zeal? Will it be myself? My glory? My opportunities? My passions? My platform? My name?

Or instead, will I choose zeal for the Lord? Will I go the other way and choose zeal for *His glory, His Heart, and His will?* Will I choose to burn in union with Him for *His bride, His House, and His Name*?

Choose wisely—preserve your eternal reward. Choose *zeal for the Lord and His house*. Choose to make a mark on eternity.

3. They will be loyal to His heart and His design for His house

The third marking I see on a rising generation of worship reformers is the mark of covenanted loyalty. They will be the ones to re-establish His heart and His vision for His house. It is evident that Jesus had a vision for His house that was quite lost on the religious regime of His day. As He kicked over tables, He clearly communicated this vision in one simple statement, shouting, *"My house will be a house of prayer for all nations."* Remember, Jesus came from the Father and clearly knew what His Father's house was supposed to look like, feel like, and be known as. He was acutely aware how its God designed purpose was being sabotaged and distorted in that moment.

If in all of our Christian building activities, we have never asked ourselves what a house of "prayer" actually is or what distinguishing marks it should embody, we really *need to*. It was clearly of immense importance to Jesus.

I don't claim to have a full revelation on this, but I do know the heart of prayer is connection and relationship. To me a house of prayer is simply a place of holy connection between God and man. It's a tent of meeting, a house of intimacy where men and women, lost and redeemed alike, can draw near and encounter the Living God. Houses of prayer are where those seeking God and those God is seeking, can both be found. They are houses of devotion, covenant, truth and encounter. Most importantly, they are houses of *His presence*.

Everything we do as leaders of God's spiritual house of prayer, is to minister purely to the Lord and facilitate that sacred connection between God and His people—those He's drawn to Himself and those He is drawing. This is what the world is starving for. *This is what the church is starving for.* Places where they can encounter the real, true, liberating, redeeming, healing, presence of God. We are not, nor will we ever be, in the Christian entertainment business. We are only in the business of connecting lost and dying people to the life, hope, and true substance of Jesus and leading them on into His way of life.

We cannot forget that the houses of worship we build are not our houses, *they are His.* And as such, they are subject to His vision and His design. If we fail to carry Jesus' vision for His house, to keep it before us as our treasured assignment, we will in turn let almost every pagan practice right through its doors. It doesn't take much discernment to see we've already done this on so many levels.

We need a generation of leaders who will again weigh everything they do against the plumb line of *His decrees and desires* and stand unwaveringly loyal to *His design.* We cannot think to hide behind the excuse of, "Well Lord, that's just how everyone was doing church in those days!" Our job was never to follow popular church structures or formats, *it was to build kingdom communities full of kingdom disciples.* We are responsible to build His kingdom on the earth, not ours—to adhere to His blueprints for His house, not the ones of our choosing.

Not only are we meant to carry God's vision for His house, *we are destined to become its visible witness*—redeemed to be a temple of His indwelling presence and a living point of connection between heaven and earth.

My brothers and sisters, you are called to be so much more than a machine that spits out three to five popular worship songs on a Sunday morning. You were born to be so much more than a pretty voice or a skilled musician. *You are called to be a house of prayer,* a living, breathing, human being, who through the power of the cross and the spilled blood of Jesus, are now connected to God the Father and have become a walking encounter with His presence.

Your assignment is not as small as *singing.* Your assignment is to release the tangible reality of *what you're singing* into the atmosphere, and to bring people into an encounter with the power and glory of God.

4. They will not hesitate to reform and cleanse His house

The fourth marking on a worship reformer is a person who won't hesitate to do what needs to be done. They will not be reluctant to pay the price that executing something in righteousness will inevitably cost. The Lord speaking through Jeremiah 4:1-2 states,

> *If you remove your detestable things from my presence, and do not waver...*

I want to emphasize the importance of not wavering in this moment. There was no wavering or hesitation in Jesus as He cleansed the temple and there can be no wavering or hesitation in us now.

However, before we zealously race out to kick over tables, we need to realize this work does not begin in someone else's life or ministry—this cleansing work begins *within us.* The only reason why Jesus had any power to bind the strongman is because He wasn't bound Himself. Before we are qualified to remove the splinter from our brother's eye, we must deal with the *plank in our own*. This much-needed reform begins when we start addressing the areas of compromise within our own hearts, confessing our own sins, and repenting in deep humility and brokenness for all the ways we have turned His house of prayer into something that no longer reflects His heart or intention.

I invite you to go on this journey of cleansing the internal temple of your own heart. To walk around the "walls" of your internal city just as Nehemiah did long ago and examine their condition. Ask yourself:

Where are they in a state of disrepair?

Where are they compromised?

Where have they been broken down?

Where am I addicted to the praise of man?

Where am I crippled by the fear of man?

Where is selfish ambition still lurking in the shadows?

Where is bitterness, unforgiveness, jealousy, offense, gossip, slander, or malice still at work within me? Are there high places in the corners of my heart? Is there sensuality, pornography and sexual sin polluting its inner chambers? Is there perverse and unclean talk corrupting my mouth?

The mystery of the ages is that the temple of the living God is no longer a building, *it's a people*. It's you and me. The saints are the living stones God is building into a spiritual house.

Paul, speaking to the Corinthians, lays out our cleansing assignment in no uncertain terms:

> *What agreement has the temple of God with idols? For we are the temple of the living God; as God said,*
>
> *"I will make my dwelling among them and walk among them, And I will be their God, and they shall be my people. Therefore, go out from their midst and be separate from them says the Lord, and touch no unclean thing; then I will welcome you, and I will be a father to you,*
>
> *And you shall be sons and daughters to me, says the Lord Almighty."*
>
> *Since we have these promises, beloved, let us cleanse ourselves from every defilement of body and spirit, bringing holiness to completion in the fear of God.*
>
> 2 Corinthians 6:16-7:1

As the Holy Spirit reveals and convicts, begin the glorious work of restoration by clearing out all that is despicable and polluting— *all that has grieved His heart*. Feel the pleasure of the Lord break out over your life as you do!

Allow the weight and mystery of God's indwelling presence to once again create a fresh tremble in your spirit and inspire a deeper journey of wholehearted consecration. This personal, cleansing work is the first and most important step in the great work of reformation God is calling us to in the heart of worship and the life of the church.

BECOMING WHOLEHEARTED
CHAPTER 4

There is a glorious life God designed you to live. A life of immeasurable freedom, joy and deep communion. *A wholehearted life.* A life where every part of the masterpiece He designed you to be fires together in a powerful unison of singular purpose. God designed you to live *whole* before Him. Undivided. Completely and utterly given over to *one thing.* One Glorious Father, Son, and Holy Spirit. A life where His rule and reign, His authority and Word, His affection and love, reside in you without conflict, without rival, and without interference.

The wholehearted life is unequivocally the best life. There is not even a distant contender.

But if this is true, why do so many of us live in such a different reality? Why do so many of us live compartmentalized, fractured, conflicted and dualistic lives? Why do so few take the path to becoming wholehearted? I believe it's because one significant obstacle stands in the way: *our death.*

Becoming wholehearted requires a death we resist dying, and a full surrender we resist yielding. To become wholehearted in everything we do is the greatest challenge many of us will face. It certainly was for me. But it was also the most powerful thing I have ever done. The day I decided to surrender everything and live wholeheartedly for the Lord, was the day everything changed. It was the turning point of my entire life.

THE LONG ROAD TO THE NARROW GATE

Like all of my journeys, this one was not quick or painless. I describe this process as the slow, agonizing, frequently resisted path towards giving God the one thing He desired most: *myself.* My whole self. I wanted to give Him something less than that. Something more convenient. Something that afforded me a little bit more flexibility and liberty to pursue the other things I wanted. I'm not a quitter and I came packaged with an extraordinary amount of stubbornness. So, the hardest thing I have ever had to do, is *give up.* Surrender. Stop resisting. Stop fighting. And *simply let GOD possess me.*

C.S. Lewis says it best: "*The terrible thing, the almost impossible thing, is to hand over your whole self—all your wishes and precautions—to Christ.*"³ Many of us are so accustomed to living a divided life that we struggle to even imagine what it would be like to have a "united heart" in place of the constant, internal war zone of conflicting desires, emotions and polarized ambitions. This condition best describes me during my late teens and early twenties. My heart was *not whole.* It was a fierce and frequent battleground of competing desires. I couldn't stand the thought of living a normal life. The thought of spending my days working a 9-5 job just to fund a mortgage and a minivan felt like personal death to my spirit.

I was driven along by a deep need for significance and status, and I began to attach those needs to any dream carrying the hope of satisfaction. I wanted a life filled with things I was passionate about and music had become my all-consuming passion. So, the dream of making it "big" in the mainstream world of music was born and quickly became my obsession and guiding light. I started a band when I was seventeen and my band mates and

I *gave* ourselves to this dream. We wrote dozens of songs, did who knows how much damage to our ears rehearsing in a garage every week, booked gigs at any coffee shop or club that would have us, and scraped together what little money we had to fund cheap, terrible recordings. We were starry-eyed and determined to make it.

We poured five years of our lives into this dream, but the whole time I could never shake the wrestle—this gnawing feeling inside of me that this wasn't quite it. It was deeply annoying. Somehow, I could still sense a call of God on my life and it terrified me. My dreams and passions had so subtly and powerfully become the source of my life and hope, I was paralyzed at the thought of surrendering them. I just knew that if I gave my full "yes" to God, I would find myself being shipped off to serve in some foreign, distant land. I was raised in church. I knew how these stories played out!

As horrible as it sounds, I just didn't want to spend the next ten years of my life living in some crude, makeshift shelter and working as a missionary. Now, I would leap at the opportunity. But back then, I just wanted to make music and be famous.

And yes, I do realize how terribly shallow that is. But that's the honest truth.

THE STORY OF MY DEATH

I tried everything to appease the nagging knowing in my spirit that I was serving myself and not the Lord. I tried the whole bartering with God thing, "*God, if you make ME famous, I will make YOU famous*" kind of deal. Of course, I worded my prayers in a much less overt way, cloaking them in deeply poetic and sincere language—as one does. Because you see, *I did love God. I did desire to serve Him. I just couldn't give Him everything.* So, I lived in this semi-tormented, un-surrendered state for a five-year period, trying to serve God but mainly just serving my dream of becoming a rock star.

The more time went on, the more confused I became about it all. I realized I was enslaved to my idea of "life." Even though it began to make me miserable, I clung to it. I resisted death. Somehow, dying to myself and giving up my dream still felt like a worse fate. But God, in His love and mercy, *kept inviting me to die.* I remember the night when it all came to a head. I had dropped in to visit my parents and the conversation quickly became an argument as my Dad confronted me yet again with the truth of my rebellion. I can still remember him saying, *"Son you're going ninety miles an hour down this road and you and I both know it may not be what the Lord has for you."* He implored me to at least seek godly counsel.

I left that night hurt and enraged. I nearly crashed my car I was so angry. But even angry I couldn't shake the truth of his words. So more out of spite than submission, I set up meetings with three pastors to seek "godly counsel." The first two meetings were fine, and the pastors simply encouraged me to keep following the Lord in my pursuits. The third pastor however, a beautiful, faithful man of God by the name of Jim Fredericks, thoughtfully listened to me. He never answered my questions, but instead asked me to answer his.

And somehow, as he began to poke and prod my "belief" systems with his questions, *I began to see the lie.* The lies I believed about God and the lies I believed about living a "normal" life.

I left that meeting broken. I can't even explain why, but I was finally ready to surrender. Come what may, I was finally ready to give up and die. And I did exactly that. I gave up my band, my dreams, my passions, my hopes. I put it all on the altar and I surrendered to God. I would love to tell you I was immediately met by angels and panoramic visions of heaven, but I wasn't. Instead, I was just miserable, mourning the loss of my "life" and still confused as to why I had to give it all up.

But I began to notice something creep into my soul over the ensuing weeks and months. I remember the night it dawned on me: "*I think this sensation I'm feeling...I think it's...I think it's peace!*" It had been so long since I'd felt peace. So long that I could barely find the language to articulate the feeling. I began to realize *that God was at work within me*. So, with a little more conviction this time, I surrendered even deeper to Him.

I began to pray for the first time ever, "*Not my will for my life, but Yours be done.*"

That simple prayer changed the entire course of my life. I hadn't written a worship song in over five years, but all of a sudden, a new sound of worship began to flow out of me. I immediately noticed these new songs were quite distinct from the previous ones I'd tried to write. They didn't sound forced or contrived or like a knock off of someone else's worship song. They had power, depth, and a weight of conviction that hadn't been there before. Something had shifted in me. I was no longer internally divided. My heart had become *whole* before the Lord and began to be *filled* with His song.

A DEATH PRECEDES A RESURRECTION

In the late 80s, the movie *The Princess Bride* was released and quickly became a cult classic. In the movie, the hero is tortured and "dies." His friends take him to the local witch doctor and instead of being pronounced dead, he is pronounced *"mostly"* dead. This always brought about a few laughs. But I find this *"mostly"* dead condition to be quite common amongst Christians. Many walk around in an almost zombie like state of partial surrender, living half-hearted in everything they do. Not only is this tragic, it is quite *costly* to the advancement of the kingdom. Why? Because we *need* resurrection power and life.

But here's the catch: *resurrection only happens to dead people.* The living don't need it.

Paul was not being poetic when he wrote to the Romans in chapter 6:3-4:

> *Or don't you know that all of us who were baptized into Christ Jesus were baptized into his death? We were therefore buried with him through baptism into death in order that, just as Christ was raised from the dead through the glory of the Father, we too may live a new life.*

The tricky part about the Christian life is that before you can experience Christ's resurrection power and new life, you must first be united with Him *in His death*. I find so many people attempting unity with Christ in His resurrection and trying to bypass unity with Him in His death. We have desired to skip "Gospel 101" and jump straight into "Gospel 201." But you can't get to 201 without 101. You must first embrace your cross, the absolute and total denial of yourself, before you can taste the life He offers on the other side.

As Dietrich Bonhoeffer put it:

"When Christ calls a man, he bids him come and die."[4]

In today's "Christianity," there are so many ideologies being used as theological shortcuts through the cost of discipleship—a myriad of ways to circumvent the way of the cross. But in reality, there are no shortcuts. So many try to propagate their vision and dreams as "kingdom pursuits," but if you look closely, it is easy to see they are self-serving at their core and rooted in selfish ambition, not sacrifice.

When I read the Gospels, I read that following Jesus means to surrender *everything*. He did not mince His words or cushion them when He said, *"If anyone would come after me, let him deny himself and take up his cross daily and follow me"* (Luke 9:23). Paul's words to the Galatians also ring with this truth: *"I have been crucified with Christ. It is no longer I who live, but Christ who lives in me"* (Galatians 2:20). There is no shortage of scriptures that clearly lay out the stipulations, demands, and costs of discipleship.

If the call doesn't require you to lay your life down, it's less than the call of Jesus. If the call doesn't cost you everything you have to obtain it, it's less than the call of the gospel.

SURRENDER AND AUTHORITY

One of the greatest missing marks on so many worship leaders today is the mark of spiritual authority. I believe this is directly connected to our individual level of surrender. The spiritual authority a believer's life was meant to carry only comes through complete and total abandonment of oneself to God. You can see evidence of this authority resting on any believer who is ready and willing to die for what they believe in. There is a spiritual weightiness that comes on a people who are only alive for one thing—*the glory of God*. A compromised, divided, half-hearted people will never carry it. It rests solely on those whose hearts have become single in their focus and undivided in their passion and pursuit.

When Jesus tells us to count the cost of discipleship, He means it. There is a great cost. There's a death. And no, it's never fun to die. *But too few talk about what waits on the other side.* Too few talk about the power of the resurrection that waits to flow through those willing to forsake their lives and wholeheartedly follow Jesus. I know whatever authority and creativity has flowed through me the past two decades can all be traced back to that initial moment of total surrender.

Remember, God has no desire to keep you dead. He only wants to kill the thing that's killing you and infuse you with His own *resurrection power, authority, and life.*

WHOLEHEARTED WORSHIP

When it comes to worship, becoming wholehearted is everything. God has never been interested in anything less than our whole hearts, and He is worthy of nothing less than our undivided love. He is a *jealous God*. He refuses to share His people with other gods, lovers, or pursuits. *He is the God who makes covenant with His people*. He is not idolatrous or polygamous. He is faithful, loyal, and true and fiercely desires a people, just as the apostle Peter wrote, "*for His own possession.*" A wholehearted, wholly devoted people.

In her classic work, *My All For Him*, Basilea Schlink so clearly captures the desire of God:

> *Because He loves us so dearly, He longs to have the whole of us. Jesus gave Himself unreservedly for us. Now He yearns for us to give ourselves completely to Him, with all that we are and have, so that He can truly be our first love. To offer Jesus anything less than this first love is of little value to Him. So long as our love for Him is a divided love, so long as family, possessions, and the like mean more to us than He does, then so long will He consider our love not to be genuine. Indeed, Jesus will not enter into a covenant of love with one whose love is divided, for a covenant of this nature requires a full, mutual love. How Jesus yearns for our love. But because our love is so precious to Him, He waits for our wholehearted commitment to undivided love.* [6]

To give your wholehearted commitment of undivided love *is your greatest act of spiritual worship* because it is the greatest thing God desires. Romans 12:1 makes this clear:

> **I appeal to you therefore, brothers, by the mercies of God, to present your bodies as a living sacrifice, holy and acceptable to God, which is your spiritual act of worship.**

Without surrender, there is no worship. Without sacrifice there is no offering, nothing for fire to fall on. Reformation, revival, awakening and fire falling, are all just conference buzz words that will remain unrealized until someone is willing to lay their life down. We are in desperate need of worship leaders who are filled with the *fire and fragrance of Jesus*. But this is only possible when our whole lives are habitually placed on the altar.

There is a spiritual authority waiting to be released on the earth, a pending glory and a holy fire. But it waits for the wholehearted ones to rise.

The ones who can truthfully declare, *"To live is Christ, and to die is gain"* (Phillipians 1:21).

FOR THE JOY

You cannot die well without a joy set before you. There is unspeakable freedom and joy waiting for those who will forsake all others, give up their lives, and surrender their whole hearts to one Lord and Master. Something changes inside of you when you begin to give yourself completely to Jesus—making His will and desires the first priority of your life.

When you begin to steward a heart solely after Him, one of the first things you're bound to notice is that heaven will begin to *respond to you.* I can promise you, when you realize heaven has taken notice of your life, decision and consecration, there will be no turning back. All the applause of man, status, notoriety, lesser dreams and ambitions, will all fade to black. They will seem as if nothing and of no importance. *No glory on earth can remotely touch the glory of heaven and the feeling of God's delight as it washes over you.*

I know there are multitudes of captive creatives who are currently imprisoned by their needs, dreams, desires, selfish ambitions, insecurities, internal emptiness, and the seduction of fame. You may be among them.

I too know what it's like to be bound by these things.

But I also know what it's like to be *completely* free of them.

And I'm writing this to tell you, *there is freedom.* Freedom in the way of Jesus. Freedom in the laying down of one's life and complete surrender. Freedom in the cross!

Freedom in the letting go of all earthly and selfish ambition.

Freedom in walking through the narrow gate of surrender and covenant; denying yourself and pledging full, undivided allegiance to Jesus. *The freedom of first love.*

Walk through those freedom gates and you will find a paradise of beauty, newness, life, creativity, purpose and abundance on the other side—the freedom and joy of a wholehearted life.

If you have never fully surrendered your life to the Lord, what's stopping you? I urge you to put this book down and get on your knees. Give Jesus the one thing He's really longing for. *Give Him your whole self.* Your whole life. Don't hold anything back. Place it all on the altar.

And watch. Fire will begin to fall.

LAND OF YOUR DREAMS
CHAPTER 5

We live in a time where dreams are celebrated and encouraged, and I praise God for that! We need dreamers who will partner with heaven and allow the dreams of God for their cities, regions, churches, industries and enterprises to flow through them like never before. The dreams God has placed inside of us operate like seeds of hope; when planted in the earth through wisdom, they grow and release His redemptive purposes. Manifested God-dreams are the salt and light of the earth, dispelling darkness and arresting corruption wherever they travel and in anyone they touch.

But this is also why the dreams within us are such a frequent spiritual battle ground.

The land of your dreams is a land rich with heavenly promise but not without its snares and pitfalls. I often see so much confusion in believers over the dreams bound up in their hearts and how they're to steward and manifest them. My dreams were once my idols. They were the things keeping me from surrender, furthering my disconnection from God, and the main obstacle to me living a wholehearted life. So, you can imagine a bit of my conflict when I was later introduced to the idea of dreaming with God. I could feel the life of the Spirit on it, but I honestly didn't know what to do. I had no desire to fall back into the same trap I had just escaped from. So, I asked God for wisdom on this and I believe He gave me a little piece of insight I will share with you.

I pray this little piece of revelation will help many navigate these waters well.

SANCTIFIED AND UN-SANCTIFIED DREAMS

This may be far too simplistic of a reduction, but I find dreams generally fall into two categories: sanctified and un-sanctified. Sanctified dreams are dreams birthed out of spiritual adoption, the fullness of intimacy with the Father, and a surrendered connection to the Holy Spirit. Un-sanctified dreams are dreams birthed out of the flesh, spiritual orphanhood, and a lack of intimacy, identity and connection to the Father. The distinguishing mark between a sanctified dream and an un-sanctified dream is almost always *its birthplace*. A dream birthed in complete, surrendered, intimate communion with God, is sanctified. A dream birthed out of an orphaned, disconnected, self-centered, ambitious place, is un-sanctified. In summary, your dreams will only be as healthy as your level of surrender and intimacy with God.

"But what about all these desires inside of me?" you may ask. "Who else but God put them there and how can pursuing them not be His will?" These are great questions and the same ones I had to wrestle with. Let me begin by affirming the truth: you were not born a blank slate. You are a created being and your deep longings and unique giftings do indeed speak to the purpose and design of your Maker.

The Lord put music and rhythm inside of my bones. When I discovered music for myself as a 12-year-old boy I literally felt a convergence with the divine; it felt like a holy exchange. I knew instinctively that music was going to be much more than an occasional hobby or relaxing pastime. *It electrified my whole being.* It possessed me and moved me in *unspeakable ways.* It was abundantly evident to me and to others that God had *marked* me for music.

However, this did not mean that every musical pursuit from that point on was a *sanctified one.* Far from it! The same is true for you. It doesn't take the gift of wisdom to know that every dream you dream is not necessarily birthed by God or something dreamed *with Him.* Just because God has marked your heart with something doesn't mean that your every attempt at its expression is His will. As John Wimber, the founder of the Vineyard Movement once said, *"The way in is the way on."*

Has God planted hopes and dreams inside of you? Yes! Has He wired you creatively and gloriously for good, world changing, works? Yes! But the doorway to their glorious fulfillment is first and foremost unification with Jesus in His death and an ongoing, daily *yielding* to His will as you follow the leading of His Spirit.

I can tell you first hand that attempting to dream *with* God before your life source *is* God, will only lead you down the path to ruin.

It's obvious to me now that my young adult dreams of rock stardom were un-sanctified, but *not* because the dream itself was un-sanctified. It lacked sanctity because it wasn't birthed *with Him,* it was birthed apart from Him. This un-sanctified dream came from a deep hole in my heart that was longing for significance and recognition but trying to derive it from the wrong source. Looking back, there isn't a doubt in my mind this un-sanctified dream would have wrecked my life, my family, and my future. If I had somehow made it in mainstream music as a twenty-two-year-old man, I would now be divorced and an addict...or worse. Instead, through surrender, I not only saw the fulfillment of dreams God placed inside of me, but also their fulfillment resulted in tremendous blessing to my family and established my future instead of thwarting it.

GOD DREAMS

If you already know you're walking in a God dream, let me exhort you with a word of caution. Even God dreams, those dreams initially birthed in a sanctified place, can become un-sanctified if you begin to move outside of intimacy and surrender and seek to control the momentum and outcome. Most of us have heard the story of Abraham and Ishmael. When Abraham sought to accomplish the promise of the Lord through his own doing, he created pain, division and mess. Even when Abraham received God's fulfillment of His promise in Isaac, God tested his heart and asked Abraham to sacrifice the very thing He promised him. This is extreme, but the reason is clear: nothing else can be allowed to live on the throne of our hearts. Not a prophecy. Not a promise. For your sake, God can't and won't allow it.

It will shipwreck your life, not establish it.

A dream birthed in surrender to the Spirit can never be brought to fruition through the control of our flesh. I have found the moment requiring the *greatest surrender* is the moment God begins *fulfilling* our dreams. I'm not sure why, but our tendency *is almost always to assume control when that happens.* In reality, that's the worst thing we can do. Most of us are aware of the great surrender required in failure, but an even greater surrender is required in success. Perhaps, if we can learn this simple truth, the bell curve and inevitable decline that history has all but etched in stone over every move of God, can be changed.

WHAT'S DRIVING ME?

I'm amazed at how many self-awareness tools we can be surrounded by, but still remain blissfully unaware of the underlying forces driving our choices and decisions. Dreams are powerful revealers and powerful drivers in our lives. They can show us things that often remain hidden. If you have never taken a hard look at your dreams, I invite you to do so. Consider it a kindness to yourself as it could save you years of frustration, pain and heartache. Don't be afraid to examine your dreams and ambitions and ask yourself:

"What's driving me? What's driving all this? If I'm honest, how pure is my root motivation? Does it flow from a sincere desire to live fully and wholeheartedly for the Lord? Is it duplicitous in any way? Is it rooted in surrendered intimacy? Or is it rooted in something else?"

If you really want this to be effective, ask the Holy Spirit to show you what's truly going on in your heart. I know He will help you. If you're married, ask your spouse. Many times, they are able to see things in your heart that you're not able to. If you're single, seek wise counsel in the form of Spirit-filled people who love you and will speak truth to you.

Maybe the Lord will show you that you are right on track and encourage you to stay the path. Maybe He will reveal a small course correction, incorrect timing, a misguided approach or a bit of broken thinking. Or maybe He will show you a complete reset is necessary and invite you to lay the dream down entirely. If He asks you to do that, find courage in Abraham's response. He was willing to sacrifice His son because He remembered one very important thing: *God can raise the dead.*

Whatever you do, don't fight Him. *Yield.* Remember God is not trying to rob you, He's working to establish you. The only things that are truly safe are the things you entrust to Him. The only way to bear fruit is to remain in an abiding connection to Him. Your dreams are something God desires to do *with* you, every step of the way. They are the history He wants to build *with* you and the history He wants to shape *through* you. It was all meant to lead you to Him, deepen your connection to Him, increase your faith in Him, your delight in Him, your joy, your love and your worship.

A fulfilled dream without Jesus is simply unfulfilling—utterly empty and void. But the smallest dreams you do *with* Jesus will bring you infinitely more happiness than the greatest dreams you accomplish without Him.

If you have never surrendered your dreams to Him, don't hesitate. Don't waste another day in disconnection. Give God all your dreams. Share them with Him. Submit them to Him. Place them in His hands. *Start enthroning Him in the land of your dreams.* One very practical way to do this is to learn to pray in all things. Prayer is an act of surrender and dependence. Pray before any vision casting, strategizing, planning, brainstorming or dreaming sessions. Pray at the beginning. Pray in the middle. Pray at the end.

Commit all your ways to Him. Let Him lead you and establish the dreams of your heart and the work of your hands.

BORN OF THE SPIRIT

CHAPTER 6

Without question, the greatest need we have in this hour is for men and women who are full of the Holy Spirit. We are not lacking gifted singers, communicators, songwriters, song leaders, or massive corporate songs. They abound more than ever. What we desperately lack is the mighty presence and power of the Spirit flowing through yielded vessels. The Holy Spirit *makes all the difference.* I'm convinced that even the most unskilled and unqualified person, *if they are yielded to the Holy Spirit,* can accomplish far more than an army of people possessing all the natural gifting and charisma in the world.

We are in desperate need of true *worship leaders.* The difference between a song leader and a worship leader, *is the Holy Spirit.* Almost anyone can play four chords and lead people in a singable chorus. But true worship leading is a Spirit empowered activity. It is learning to lead and sing in the Spirit, with the Spirit, and by the Spirit. Paul's writing to the Philippians in 3:3 makes this clear, *"For we...who worship by the Spirit of God and glory in Christ Jesus."* Without the presence and empowerment of the Holy Spirit, our worship doesn't get very far off the ground. It is the touch of the Spirit on a song and on a leader that causes hearts to open and releases the worship and fragrance God's heart is longing for.

There has not been a single holy and anointed worship moment I've stepped into that wasn't directly connected to following what I felt the Holy Spirit impress upon my heart. The very first time I led the song "Our Father" was under the prompting of the Holy Spirit. It was forty-five minutes into a Sunday night worship service. The set was going terribly, and I just wanted it to be over. But I remember throwing up a half-hearted prayer, "*We wait for You to come and show Your glory here today...*" and then I basically gave up. But as my co-lead began to sing the next song, something began to happen in the room.

His glory began to *physically manifest.*

We couldn't see it at first but all of a sudden, the atmosphere changed, and the air became electrified in the room. There was a stirring in the crowd. The only song I could think to sing in that moment was a song I barely knew. We hadn't rehearsed it and it wasn't on the set list, but I couldn't shake the feeling I was supposed to lead it. So, before I could even remember if I knew all the lyrics or not (which I didn't), I gathered my courage and began to sing out softly, *"Our Father...in heaven...hallowed be Your name..."*

As we began to sing that song, His glory began to visibly increase in the room. I will never forget watching the air in front of my face begin to shimmer and sparkle in the most bewildering way. It's one thing to sing, *"Let heaven come,"* but it's quite another to watch His glory physically manifest before your very eyes, *while you're singing it.*

For a brief moment, I got to experience what worship was always meant to feel like. As God's glory began to take center stage, the stage I was on began to disappear. There were no longer any "special" people with "special" titles in the room. Everyone was simply a worshiper. Every eye was lifted towards heaven and caught up in awe and wonder.

NEVER GOING BACK

Life with the Holy Spirit will ruin you for the ordinary. When you taste what's available through simple, submissive partnership to His leadings, you will never want to do life any other way. His leadership consistently transforms the most common interactions into full blown encounters, the most average worship sets into heavenly moments, and the most ordinary people into extraordinary leaders. Leaning into His voice is what opens the door to supernatural power. When the Holy Spirit comes upon you, you will do things, say things, sing things, and write things that are far beyond your natural giftings, abilities, or capacity.

If I could divide my "ministry" into two eras, the first one would be me largely ignorant of the Holy Spirit's leadership or how to follow Him. The second era would be marked by an intentional pursuit of His leading and consistent obedience to whatever I felt Him prompt me to do or sing. There really is no comparing the two eras. In the first era, I saw very little spiritual activity. In the second era, I saw more than I ever dreamed was possible. The first era was filled with lots of sweet, beautiful, thirty-minute worship sets. I was satisfied with just getting a chance to lead and sing; satisfied with the church program, four to five songs, a great band, solid preaching and lunch afterwards.

But *everything* began to change when I saw the Holy Spirit get involved.

I began to notice certain people had something I lacked—*a real sensitivity to the Holy Spirit.* They were able to recognize when God wanted to do something in a meeting, and when they acted on it, *everything changed.* We went from doing nice, normal church to the weight of His presence dropping like a bomb in the room and people getting radically touched, delivered and set free. As I witnessed heaven break in time after time just because someone was sensitive to the Holy Spirit and did what He asked, a fire began to *burn* inside of me. I became desperately hungry to know the Holy Spirit in the same way. I knew I could no longer afford to live ignorant of His voice and leadership, and I began to cry out for Him to reveal Himself to me.

He is faithfully answering that prayer to this day.

THE PRESENCE IS A PERSON

Everything with God begins and ends in relationship. The Holy Spirit is no different. His power is not released when we figure out the right formulas, the right performances, or the right religious rituals. His power is released when we begin to walk in right understanding and right relationship with Him.

I know that "Presence" has become the new language for the Holy Spirit in the church. Maybe that phrasing has made us feel safer or has felt more palatable. It has been *"presence this"* and *"presence that"* or *"Did you feel the presence on that?"* and *"There was so much presence in the room!"*

I've used this language as much as anybody and I'm far from against it. However, it is vital we understand that the Presence is not some abstract, mystical force.

The "Presence" is a Person.

This may seem very basic and elementary, but if we don't keep the "presence" connected to the Person of the Holy Spirit, *we miss the invitation to know Him and to move with Him.* He is not a mist, a cloud, a vibe, or an atmosphere—*He is a person.*

When we say, *"The presence came so strong!"* it means the Person of the Holy Spirit *"came so strong."* Just like my "presence" is never disconnected from my person, neither is His. We do very harmful things when we de-humanize people and we endanger ourselves in the same way when we impersonalize His Person. An abstract "presence" doesn't have a heart, feelings, desires, sensitivity, grief, awareness, nearness, sovereignty or holiness; *but the Holy Spirit most certainly does.* When we speak about Him, we should always seek to do so in a way that honors Him as a Person.

Many of us have been tragically trained to see the Holy Spirit as an optional, extra-Christian "experience"—reserved only for the charismatics or super spiritual. Many more have unknowingly limited Him to a one-time encounter that happened during an altar call, a ministry time, or a youth camp. But He is infinitely more than that! *He is the abiding relationship every believer was meant to walk in every day of their lives.* The One given to us by our Father to lead us, guide us, fill us, convict us, comfort us, teach us, commune with us, and empower us to fulfill our purpose here on the earth. We were *never* meant to do life, ministry or leadership without Him.

So many people have *encountered* the Holy Spirit, but too few have learned to *walk with Him.*

IN STEP WITH THE SPIRIT

Following the Holy Spirit isn't about "ministry time" moments at church; *it's about an entirely new way of living.* To experience an encounter with the Holy Spirit is wonderful, but it was only meant to be the starting point of the journey, not the destination. One of the most frequently quoted scriptures in the Bible is Paul's words to the Galatians telling them, *"If we live by the Spirit, let us also keep in step with the Spirit."* Learning to keep in step with the Spirit may sound like a very simple thing (and in truth it is), but it is deeply challenging. Numerous people and churches fail in their attempts to *"keep in step with the Spirit"* because they underestimate just how radical of a reset is required.

The distinctive quality about Christian leadership is that it's less about *leading* and it's more about *following.* I've read leadership book after leadership book and I'm so grateful for the wisdom they've imparted. But before any of us are called to lead, we're first and foremost called to *follow.* The way to follow Jesus this side of heaven is to follow the One He sent to help us when He went away, *the Holy Spirit.* If we are to become true spiritual leaders, then our highest aim is to become Spirit-filled and Spirit-led. Our greatest assignment every day is to be a people who stay in step with the Spirit.

In this, all I can share with you is my own journey. I've never struggled to step up and lead, but I've certainly struggled to follow and submit. I typically like being in control. I like having a road map. I used to have all my worship sets meticulously mapped out. I knew where they started, where they ended, and everything in between. So, when I decided to go on this journey of learning how to keep *"in step with the Spirit"* I had to release all of that control and fiercely commit to a brand new posture. This wasn't a small adjustment to my spiritual life; it was a *radical re-orientation* of it. I had to firmly embrace my new position as "subordinate leader" at all times and in all things. I had to wage daily war against my independent nature because subordinate leaders *do not* move independently. I had to break with all my old ways of preparing, leading and executing and step into a brand new way of surrendered co-laboring.

Following the Holy Spirit is not isolated to your "spiritual" assignments, it involves the whole of your life and decision-making process. It's cultivating a heart that's continually seeking to be led by Him and willingly obedient to His voice. It's learning to invite the Holy Spirit into the dialogue—to continually commune and consult with Him. As I've learned to converse with the Holy Spirit, I've discovered how much He has to say about my life, my church, my assignments, my set lists, my wife, my kids, my finances, my relationships, my eating and drinking habits, my daily rhythms...*all of it.*

Early on in this process, I was feeling slightly appalled after realizing how little I relied on the Holy Spirit or asked for His help and guidance. I remember sheepishly acknowledging to Him, "You've probably been waiting for me to bring you in on the conversation for a long time now, haven't You?" I couldn't help but remember how frustrating it was when leaders under me would go about executing things and assuming they knew what I thought or wanted *without ever interacting or checking in with me.* Even though I'm still guilty of this from time to time, I keep repenting and contending for a posture that's continually submitted and sensitive to the Holy Spirit.

Ever since the day I made that commitment to follow the Holy Spirit no matter what, there hasn't been a single worship set that has ever gone according to plan—He's interrupted all of them (as any musician I've ever played with can attest). This used to terrify me, but now I only joyfully anticipate it. However messy the journey, I've learned that following Him always brings about *real spiritual breakthrough.*

I encourage you to commit your life and leadership to the Holy Spirit in the same way. This new surrendered way of living and leading is certainly not without its challenges, but it is far more life-giving, joy-filled, and heaven-infused than its alternative. Once that yielded, communing posture is set in you, you will find it becomes as effortless as breathing.

And you will never want to go back to the way it was before.

FULLY YIELDED

I still find it amusing how many processes I went through, skill sets I developed, leadership tools I acquired, and labor intensive seasons I waded through only to discover the key all along was *yielding to the Holy Spirit*. I mean, does anyone else find it ironic how many years of striving it takes to finally learn to give up? How long it takes to stop trying to impress and please people and *simply surrender*? Spiritual maturity is formed in someone who has learned to yield to the Holy Spirit; to wait, to listen, to hear and to obey.

The greater the yielding, the greater the power.

True spiritual power does not flow through powerful people, only surrendered ones. Only people who have chosen to become weak and emptied of their own power, will be filled with His. But that's the hurdle most of us keep balking at. Whether in fear or faithlessness, we are reluctant to bankrupt ourselves of our own power in order to be filled with His. We continually retreat to the familiar safety and security of our own proven methods.

But no yielding continues to equal no power.

There was a time when I thought the biggest obstacle to a *"demonstration of the Spirit and of power"* (1 Corinthians 2:4) in

THE RESET

the church today was rooted in theological opposition. But I've come to see the much greater issue is our wrestle with surrender and our fear of relinquishing control. Talk of surrender is popular, public example is rare. It may be an inspiring preach but it's a deeply uncomfortable reality. Surrender puts things out of our hands and out of our control. It's risky and unpredictable; especially when you don't know where it's going to take you.

I find much of the church hungers for revival, longs for a move of the Spirit, wants to see heaven invade earth, wants to see the "greater things" break out, but simultaneously fails to yield their plans, agendas, or production to the leading of the Holy Spirit. So, they see very little. We are fond of crying out *"Lord, do whatever you want to do tonight!"* in our pre-service prayer times, but week after week, we keep choosing the consistency of our programs, proven set lists, and controlled outcomes over risking to follow His voice. Week after week we choose control instead of surrender, and yet we wonder why there is no power.

Oh, how I wish we were less impressed with what we were able to accomplish in and of our own strength! We continue to be impressed with our church growth and numbers when in fact the church in the United States is in massive decline. We're impressed with our "relevant" services and hip pastors while the culture around us continues to decay into an abyss of moral chaos and injustice. How long will we stay enamored with what we can accomplish in and through our own power and remain blinded to our bankruptcy? How long until we wake up and realize our mightiest efforts are utterly feeble in comparison, and wholly give ourselves to *His ways, His plans, and His power?*

The breakthrough we are longing to see in our nations, in our cities, in our communities and in our churches is *only a breath away.*

It only takes one encounter with His mighty presence to know the hardest hearts can melt, the most crippling diseases can be healed, and the most impossible situations can shift, *at just the touch of His hand and a drop of His power.*

He is present. He is waiting. He is ready to act.

The question is, *are we ready to yield?*

TRUTH MATTERS
CHAPTER 7

Growing up, I never realized how much I took the truth for granted. I just assumed the church would always hold fast to the written Word of God because...well...that's just what churches *do*...right? *They believe the Bible.* At least that was the firm conviction my grandparents and parents held, so I just assumed it was universal. I had no idea how costly it was for the previous generations to establish and uphold Scripture as the absolute truth and plumb line for the Christian life. I definitely mistook how fragile that work really was and *how quickly it could crumble.* At present, I'm greatly sobered. I don't know if our faltering in this moment is because the war over truth has never been stronger or if the church's resistance to deception has never been weaker. Both feel true. All I know is, the necessity of the truth being seen on us and proclaimed through us, is of critical importance in this hour.

The most quoted verse on worship in the Bible records Jesus speaking to the woman at the well and declaring:

> *But the hour is coming, and is now here, when the true worshipers will worship the Father in spirit and truth, for the Father is seeking such people to worship him. God is Spirit, and those who worship him must worship in spirit and truth.* John 4:23

The first attribute of the true worshipers God is seeking, is a people who worship *"in spirit."* The second attribute is *truth*. Truth may not get nearly as much attention (particularly amongst creatives) as heart and spirit do, but Jesus' words put *equal emphasis* on its importance. It should not surprise us that God insists on being worshiped *for who He actually is*. He is not honored by ignorance or falseness. No one is. None of us appreciates being honored for who we're not.

Only *truth* has the power to honor.

If our worship lacks truth, it fails to attract, minister to, or honor the One we're worshiping.

WHAT MAKES WORSHIP, WORSHIPFUL?

Mankind has been worshiping since the beginning of time; busily crafting all manner of gods and an endless variety of accompanying religious rituals and practices for the sake of appeasing, connecting with, and entreating these same gods. The important thing to note is, whatever the worship practice may be, it's consistently *subject* to the gods themselves. Even pagan worship has understood that the only one who can determine whether an act of worship is actually "worshipful," *is the one being worshiped.* Therefore, each expression of worship must be custom tailored to the uniqueness of the god it's been aimed at.

Though the worship of our God—the One, True, Living God—is distinct in almost every way, in this, *it is the same.* Yes, He desires worship. Yes, He's seeking worshipers. But He is very *specific* about the *kind* of worship He desires and the *kind* of worshiper He's seeking. Fortunately for us, He didn't leave these specifics ambiguous or unclear. He gave us a massive book, the Bible— chock-full of revelation into who He is, what His heart longs for, and what offerings of worship are pleasing to Him.

The very simple point I'm trying to make is this: *worship is only worship if it pleases God.* It doesn't matter if it *sounds* like worship, or if it's labeled as "worship," or if it's in every "inspirational" category on iTunes; it doesn't even matter if it's taken up and sung by every worship leader in every worship service around the globe...

If God doesn't like it...it's not worship.

THE KNOWLEDGE OF GOD

All worship begins with some form of knowledge about God. The worship of God and the knowledge of God are inseparable. Without the knowledge of God, we don't have the slightest clue *how* to worship Him. We're clueless as to what He requires of us or how to bring Him something that pleases His heart. It is the knowledge of the Lord alone that gives us this insight. Without the knowledge of God, all worshipers are people fumbling about in the dark.

Revelation is what fuels and informs worship. But even with clear revelation, it amazes me how quickly we can get off track... how quickly worship can turn into something that "moves us," but *doesn't move Him.* Many times, Israel really did think God delighted in the sacrifice of bulls and sheep. Many times, they did sincerely believe He was satisfied with their religious practices instead of the posture of their hearts and lives. Time and time again God had to interrupt His people in the midst of the fervor of their religious worship activity and declare to them, "*This is NOT what I'm after!*"

Away with your noisy hymns of praise! I will not listen to the music of your harps. Instead, I want to see a mighty flood of justice, an endless river of righteous living.
Amos 5:23-24 (NLT)

I would love to think this no longer applies to us, but I'm finding we may be just as guilty. God has never been interested in a good religious show. He never will be. He's not searching for a great group of singers or a bunch of people who have perfected the ever-increasing catalogue of charismatic worship moves. I don't think He's ever looked down from heaven and said, "*Yep, there they go again. Singing and moving and swaying. Boy I just love it when they do that...*" That's never been His "thing."

What He's looking for is a people who *really know Him...* Who walk in the knowledge of *His truth*.

The prophet Hosea records the Lord Himself speaking,

For I desire steadfast love and not sacrifice, the knowledge of God rather than burnt offerings. Hosea 6:6

Without the knowledge of God, no worshiper has any assurance that their religious activities, offerings, or events are actually *pleasing to the Lord* or are the things He desires from them. Not only do a people without the knowledge of God *miss God*, they are *ruined* for the lack of it. The prophet Hosea again records the Lord speaking on this issue,

My people are destroyed for lack of knowledge; because you have rejected knowledge, I reject you from being a priest to me. Hosea 4:6

This is a sobering word to any modern-day Levite.

The question we need to ask ourselves is this: *do we know God?* Have we been spending time studying who *He's* revealed Himself to be in His Word, or have we simply been studying other people's songs, books, and social media feeds? If our songwriting is any indication, we need to spend less time living vicariously through other people's revelation and more time getting our own. We need to commit to deepening our individual knowledge of God through consistent and careful study of His Word.

THE PURPOSE OF THEOLOGY

We recently lost one of the great theologians and men of the faith in our day, J.I. Packer. I have shared his quote since the first day I read it nearly twenty years ago.

> *"Theology is for doxology and devotion— that is, the praise of God and the practice of godliness."*[5]

This is so important for worship leaders to understand: *theology is for doxology.* Meaning the whole point of studying God is to *worship God.* It's not to get puffed up, elitist and pedigreed. It's to enable us to step into a greater level of *worship.*

This lit such a fire in me when I first grasped this. All of a sudden, I realized it's the worshipers who were meant to be the *greatest theologians.* The in-depth study of the Word of God has been left to scholars and intellectuals, but it must be equally claimed by the artist, the musician, and the poet. If our assignment as worship leaders is to lead people into doxology (worship), then we've been tasked with the privilege of becoming some of the greatest theological minds of our day.

We must leave the former days of biblical ignorance and academic laziness behind us and *plunge ourselves into the Word of God*. Love and honor have no power unless they are *fueled by knowledge and revelation*. The less you know about God, the harder it is to worship Him.

The more you feast on Him, the more it gushes out of you.

TRUTH AND LOVE

Love is inherently fascinated with the object of its affection. It can't help itself. It naturally obsesses. For a lover, it's no hard or tedious task to study the one its heart loves. It's ever intrigued and always longing to make a deep search of the person or thing it loves.

Somehow, we intuitively know that making a deep impact on someone's heart requires us to *know them deeply*. Whether through positive or negative experience, anyone who has ever dated someone knows the importance of this. When that first Valentine's Day or birthday rolls around, only the ones who have thoughtfully studied their lover and brought them a gift that demonstrates insight and attentiveness to their heart, are substantially rewarded. Those who simply go with a token gift (the typical chocolate and flowers) may get away with it for a time, but if they don't deepen their study, they will cease to impact the heart.

The principle I'm driving at is this: *what you study always reveals what you love.*

Here is where we must address a disconnect in the worship community. Proverbs 19:2 says, *"Desire without knowledge is not good."* But this is so often evident among us. So many write ardent, love-sick declarations and songs to Jesus, *but so few study Him.* Something is missing. To say, "I love you Jesus!" but to have never poured over the Gospels in fascinated, devoted study of His life and words, *simply lacks conviction.* It's *hollow.* It's quite possible you are only in love with the *idea* of Him, and not who He really is. To study Him and the truth of who He is, *is the evidence of genuine love.*

This generation may be the most self-aware generation in history. We've taken every kind of personality test there is and filled our shelves and e-readers with their wisdom. We have become experts in "self-love" and "self-care" and we freely educate our friends, family, distant cousins, spouses, pets, neighbors and Facebook friends on the art and intricacy involved in "loving us" well. We know the five love languages and gladly make known which ones minister to us the most.

We have learned so much about how to love ourselves and so little about how to love the Lord.

I find myself wondering if anyone has bothered to ask God what His top love languages are? Or sought to know the depth and intricacy of His heart to the same degree we have sought to know our own? Oh, what measure of transformational power would begin to flow through a community that *treasured His words and prioritized them above all else!*

We are already living in that time where people are "lovers of self." This has been increasingly leaching into the area of worship. So, *I charge you,* be someone who stands in stark contrast to this generation. Be someone who lays down their obsession with themselves and takes up an insatiable thirst and hunger *to know Him*. Be someone full of the knowledge and revelation of His Word. Be someone who can read Psalm 119 and feel like you've found a friend.

Be someone who has so firmly placed yourself under the authority of Scripture that its authority *begins to flow through you.*

AS GOES WORSHIP, SO GOES THE CHURCH

Belinda Huang noted that "music has the power to culturally, morally, and emotionally influence our society."[6] This is not any different within the church. One of the most sobering truths about worship songs is that they're cultural carriers and influencers. They can have more power to establish culture in a church than its preaching does. I have watched this phenomenon happen through multiple movements, numerous times, and just in my short lifetime. It's not hard to see how Bethel's, Hillsong's and Elevation's worship has dramatically impacted church culture around the globe. Worship has always been the forerunner.

But this truth carries a sobering weight and responsibility with it. One could even go as far as to say: *as goes the worship movement, so goes the church*. This may not be the entire truth of the matter, but there is plenty of truth in it.

What we sing becomes cultural.

If we have eyes to see it, the modern-day worship movement has reinvented the culture of the church in our day. Some have seen this as positive and others as negative. I find the effects of the songs tend to be as healthy as the cultures of worship they spring from and the level of truth they carry. But the thing I'm really trying to draw attention to is the tremendous weight this places on worship communities to not only be cultural forerunners, but *forerunners in the truth.*

If what we sing becomes cultural, then what we sing *better be true.*

A RETURN TO THE WORD

I don't believe I'm overreacting when I say the neglect of truth and sound doctrine amongst worship communities and the church at large, has come with devastating consequences. This sin of neglect has obliterated our spiritual immune system and left us susceptible to every virus of confusion and deception. Many churches and Christian movements are increasingly allowing minds bent on sin and the justification of evil to completely twist, tame, soften and re-render the clear commands of God.

The only thing that can arrest the spiritual dullness rapidly descending upon the body of Christ and pierce us awake is the *"sword of the Spirit, which is the word of God"* (Ephesians 6:17). Scripture is *"Sharper than any double-edged sword, it penetrates even to dividing soul and spirit, joints and marrow; it judges the thoughts and attitudes of the heart"* (Hebrews 4:12).

We must understand, *Scripture is OUR judge.* Not the other way around. We're not just reading Scripture; it's *reading us.* Scripture is revealing the thoughts and attitudes of *our hearts* and exposing them to us.

I have begun to wonder if the gross empowerment and elevation of personal opinion on social media has really deluded us into thinking that our opinions hold any weight against the Word of God. I wonder if we have been so trained by a democratic, consumer driven society that we have forgotten that the kingdom of God is not a democracy, but a *theocracy*. A government in which *His Word and His Word alone stands*. We must return to our senses and *know this*: when it comes to the Word of God, the online uproar and outcry of seething, opinionated objections and dissenting votes, *has absolutely zero weight*. It doesn't matter. I'm not saying our voice doesn't matter to God. I'm simply reminding us: Dissenting against *His voice* is absolute folly.

Somehow, we keep finding new ways to insulate our hearts from the Word of God—to dismiss it, customize it, or alter it. We readily highlight, ingest, and declare the *promises* of scriptures but willfully ignore its *warnings, its judgments and its piercings*. Has history taught us nothing? When we over emphasize one aspect of the truth but neglect its *equally important* counterparts, we almost *always* end up with something heretical. Half-truths have always been the devil's method. We must open our eyes and see how he has cloaked every immoral agenda on the earth in half-truths! He is always trying to divide God's "love" from His truth and God's "goodness" from His holiness.

Our neglect of the Word of God has brought us here, but a return to it has the power to right it. *There must be a wholehearted returning to the Word of God in the church and in the worship community.* And by "returning," I mean a fresh *submission to its authority*.

In his letter to Timothy, Paul speaks of the church as "*a pillar and a buttress of truth*" (1 Timothy 3:15). A pillar and a buttress are an integral support system upholding many ancient cathedrals and buildings to this day. We need a fresh revelation that declaring the truth is not a *secondary* mission for the church, *it is a primary one*. Real love is never divorced from the truth but must speak the truth in every way.

If the church refuses to be an un-wielding support system that undergirds the truth against the onslaught of lies and deception, the church will crumble. A world that denies the truth is not a world we want to live in. *But it is on our doorstep.* We must return to the Word of God! We must hold it fast and without shame, *declare it boldly*.

"IN TRUTH"

I can say without hesitation that the single most powerful and transformational thing I've ever done, is read the Bible. Reading God's Word has literally transformed my life more than any other encounter or experience I've ever had. To this day, the more I read His Word, the more I fall in love with Him. His Word is alive, and *it will set your world on fire if you let it*.

If you will grow and deepen your knowledge of the truth, worshiping Him with the whole of your mind as well as the whole of your heart, you will notice a much greater power and authority beginning to accompany your worship— an immediate overflow of praise in your mind and heart that will flow out of you with unexpected ease. No longer will you have to "dig deep" during a spontaneous moment, or repeatedly sing the same two or three cliche phrases. If you deepen your well, your well will start to overflow.

I'll close this chapter with three simple disciplines to get you started:

First, *study the truth*.

Pour over Scripture. Fill your mind with the knowledge of who He is. Take note of every description of His heart, ways, character, attributes and glory that Scripture reveals. Learn what God likes. Discover what moves His heart and what delights His soul. Learn how He loves to be loved. Know Him!

Then, *sing the truth*.

Take all the knowledge of God you've been studying in Scripture, all the revelation He's been filling you with in regard to His heart and His ways, and then begin to sing it back to Him. Fill your private times of worship with His truth. Make singing Scripture a discipline in your life. Fill the worship sets you lead with songs of His truth. Write songs that are full of the knowledge and revelation of who He is.

Finally, *live the truth*.

Worshiping God in truth doesn't only mean study, it means doing the things He reveals to you in His Word and speaks to you in your heart. The full weight of truth is only discovered as you live it out. You are not called to be a broker of someone else's revelation or information, but someone who has personally tasted and seen for themselves and knows it to be true.

A NEW WINESKIN
CHAPTER 8

I believe the greater things we are longing to see in worship—the creative works that will carry a far weightier measure of the anointing, presence, and power of the Spirit—are waiting on new wineskins. The previous ones we created may have served a season and a purpose, but they will not take us into the future. *They will just keep ruining the wine.* We need new wineskins that will cherish His presence over profit, His glory over our own, and obedience to Him above all.

When it comes to worship songs and projects, if the end result is intended to *be worship*, then all of its processes must be birthed, saturated and sustained *in worship*. Why would we anticipate the final product carrying any measure of the Spirit's anointing if the entire creative process was anything but spiritual? Harvey S. Firestone wisely understood, "Success is the sum of details." In other words, the details matter because the details *create the sum.* There is a common saying, "The devil is in the details." But the devil is only in them because we have forgotten to enthrone *God there.*

Because we have forgotten that the details and process matter as much to God as the end result, we have unwittingly given Satan a sabotaging foothold there. We need a fresh realization that when it comes to releasing songs and records that carry the true spirit of worship, *every detail matters*. Every relationship, every record contract, every songwriter split...*matters*. Every heart, every attitude, every motive...*matters*. Music production *matters*. The purity of the musicians *matters*. The hearts of the engineers *matter*. Honor towards one another *matters*. Business models *matter*. Generosity *matters*. Above all, *love matters*.

Over the past couple of decades, I've engaged and interacted with current industry models and watched them slowly homogenize and sterilize so many anointed worship leaders and movements. We need a complete shift in our thinking. We've created models that demand *conformity* rather than *creativity*. These models serve structures and formulas instead of people. There must be a new wineskin for creating, producing and distributing worship music.

The wineskins I'm referring to here are the current music industry models and business structures. The w*ine is the people and the sound they carry*. What we need today are true, gifted *vintners* (winemakers). A true vintner's passion is never the wineskin (the structure)—their *passion is always the wine* (the people). They're not in the business of serving wineskins, they're in the business of bringing out *the best flavor and character in the wine*. Not only do they celebrate a wine's unique qualities and distinctions, they diligently work to enhance and mature them.

THE MYTH OF A "CHRISTIAN" MUSIC INDUSTRY

Before jumping into the need for new wineskins, let me briefly address the old one: the "Christian" Music industry. This model may still be useful to Christian music artists and bands, but apart from a deep work of repentance and reformation, I don't believe this industry is fit to carry and release the new sound of worship God is about to pour out. Please know these are only my personal observations and convictions. My four points are broad strokes and I have no doubt there are exceptions to what I'm about to share. And I rejoice in that!

But here are the reasons I feel the current "Christian" music industry is an unfit wineskin for the worship movement:

Lack of Kingdom Ethics and Practice: For some reason the Christian music industry never deemed it necessary to "re-invent the wheel" but chose instead to pattern itself after the secular music industry and all its brokenness. We did not create our own business model; we simply cut and pasted the world's. There is a clear command in Scripture that we ignored. Romans 12:2 states, *"Do not conform to the pattern of this world."* Scripture is clear that God cares about the administrative details, the spirit of our contracts, and our ways of doing business as Christians. How much more so when it comes to the musical expression *carrying the sole message of hope for mankind and exclusively assigned to His glory?* If it never crossed our minds that God might have a different way for us to walk in, a different set of principles and government to inform our creative, executive and distributive processes, *it should have.* As Christians, we have had two thousand years of teachings on the counter cultural nature of His kingdom, but we are still ignoring these teachings and willfully choosing to model the world's. This lack of holiness *will only continue to taint the new wine.*

Secular Leadership: Most Christians are unaware that the biggest Christian record labels are now subsidiaries of larger mainstream secular record labels—meaning they are owned and controlled by them. These mainstream labels are in turn owned by much larger media conglomerates. These "partnerships" have subtly (and not so subtly) steered the laws, the practices, and the "spirit" that now governs most Christian labels. If you're curious how the mainstream music industry came to be involved in the Christian one, there are two simple reasons. First, Christian music began to be profitable. Second, Christian labels willingly *chose* to partner with them. Although quite good for business and growth, I'm not sure how we anticipated anything distinct or holy coming from this kind of alliance. Friends, I'm a purist (surprise!) and I make no apologies for it. In my book this is a fairly straightforward matter. Fig trees don't bear grapes and bad trees don't bear good fruit. This un-equally yoked marriage will hinder *the mission of the new wine*.

Lack of Witness: I believe Scripture makes it abundantly clear that the primary assignment and joy of every Christian person (and enterprise) on this earth *is to bear witness to Jesus and glorify Him in everything we do and create*. I strongly feel the Christian music industry is missing this as its primary purpose; it is gravely lacking *true witness*. If I were to simply call it as I see it, I'd say much of the current music industry that labels itself "Christian," *is not*. In order for something to be rightly called "Christian," it *must adhere* to the model of Jesus. Let's simply call it the "music industry" and spare His name, or, conform it and pattern it after His ways and His heart. This confusion of identity and purpose will only temper *the intensity of the new wine*.

No Accountability within the Church: It's important to be aware that much of the "Christian" music industry is entirely rogue. And by "rogue" I mean it has no direct connection or subordination to any kind of church government. Outside of a few well-known worship labels *that are* connected to church movements, this industry has no accountability for its conduct or its dealings within the church. I'll just state the obvious: When anything is empowered to represent Christianity to the culture in any kind of significant way, but remains outside the church's leadership, ethics, or authority...*that's an issue.* To be a Christian is to live *accountable* to the body of Christ and the authority of Scripture. This lack of accountability in the industry creates a vulnerability to disease and corruption that *will inevitably ruin the new wine.*

I know many people will respond to these points and say, "But look at the testimonies within the industry! Look at the fruit and changed lives!" I don't discredit them in any way. They are real testimonies and I'm grateful for each and every one of them. God really does move in mysterious ways! I will forever be amazed (and perplexed) by how He continues to work through the most broken models, people and creative works. I don't know how many times this has *deeply offended* my mind. Probably as many times as I've had to remember, I'm *one of those broken, creative people God continues to work through.* It really is an amazing grace. But I think we frequently confuse God's grace with God's approval. God continuing to work through a broken system or person is just that: *a testimony of His grace,* not an indication of His approval.

That said, I really don't see the current "Christian" music industry changing in any significant way. I could fantasize about this sparking sweeping reform but...history tells me it's quite unlikely. The model is still working at some level and as long as that's the case, there will always be someone trying to keep it up and running. And there will always be genuine people doing genuine things in the midst of it and producing genuine fruit.

But this unrelenting hope continues to possess me:

If a measure of His power and purpose can flow through such broken systems and people...imagine what greater measure of His power and purpose could flow through wholehearted, consecrated ones.

This is what my heart is *longing* to see.

NEW VINEYARDS

Our mission in life isn't to figure out how to live within the broken constructs of existing enterprises; it's to build new ones on firm, biblical foundations. We must show leaders why they're so *desperately needed.* Much new wine has already been wasted on old wineskins. If we want to stop this and spare the new wine, *we have to create new wineskins.*

I'm honestly not trying to tear something down so much as I'm trying to inspire us to build something new. My heart burns to inspire and commission the true and righteous vintners to rise up and courageously plant new vineyards.

I believe the *new wineskins* will come from *new vineyards.*

Many of these future vineyards will be smaller, more homegrown and family oriented. They will be more connected to the soil, the vines and the grapes and far more holistic and pastoral in their approach. They will understand that making great wine does not begin at the harvest but begins with tending soil and roots. In most industries, bigger means better and more expensive. But in the world of wine, bigger almost always means more generic and cheap tasting.

These new vineyards may be smaller and more humble in

appearance, but that does not mean they will produce cheap wine. Far from it. The wine they produce will be *priceless*.

Endeavoring to plant a new "vineyard" is the journey the Lord has me on at present. As some of you very well know, taking a dream that's lived inside of your heart for years and working to develop it is one of the most humbling and vulnerable processes you can go through. I've had to learn a lot about faith, contentment and letting righteousness be its own reward. Most of the initial work has been tending to the soil and I find myself wishing I had more to show for my efforts.

But a few roots are going deep. Some vines are popping up. I know new wine is coming.

Establishing a "vineyard" (also known as growing a creative enterprise) is akin to embarking on a wild farming adventure. It's true that adventure is almost always synonymous with challenge and difficulty, but the reward of a righteous pursuit is always worth the overcoming. The best part about doing something in righteousness (God's way) is being able to fully surrender the results and place them in the Father's very capable hands. The pressure is not on you to deliver. What is completely devoted to Him no longer rests on your shoulders.

NEW WINE

They say necessity is the mother of invention. I believe that's because necessity makes *you hungry*. Desperate even. We have a poetic and romanticized idea of hunger and thirst, but they are not pleasant experiences. They are the result of *lack and depri-*

vation. These new vineyards won't be birthed until *we see them as a necessity.* They won't be birthed until our hearts are *breaking over the lack of new wine*! Until we are languishing for lack of a pure fragrance to Jesus rising on the earth! Until our hunger and thirst for fresh expressions of authentic, bridal love *drives us to take action.*

Is anyone else longing to experience more than what they've tasted and seen in worship thus far? Has anyone else's heart been ruined for the ordinary because they've witnessed a moment of God's glory and visitation? Is there any holy hunger for God to move in signs, wonders, miracles and salvation?

Who is leaning into the more of God right now? Because *there is more!*

I find myself dreaming of an atmosphere of worship *so full of His glory that it transforms anyone coming into it.* I see a people coming in with calloused and deadened hearts towards God but leaving fully alive to Him. I see a people coming in oppressed and harassed but leaving fully liberated. A people coming in asleep to the call of God on their lives but leaving awakened to their divine destiny. A people coming in under the weight of depression and despair but leaving in great joy and gladness! A people coming in bound by addiction and disease but leaving unshackled and free. A people coming in afflicted by bodily pain and suffering but leaving healed and restored.

My heart is crying out for a sound of worship in the earth so full of faith that the lost find themselves spontaneously crying out and confessing, "*Jesus is Lord!*" I want to see a realm of glory and power so thick and tangible that no one in the room can deny the presence of God in our midst! If a piece of cloth could come in contact with an anointed person and carry healing to the sick who touched it, then how much more could worship music release deliverance, healing and salvation wherever it's played?

I burn for this! I burn for this because I've tasted of it. I've been changed by it! I'm only here today because I came into a place of His manifest presence and glory. I came in down and out... all but spiritually dead... *but I woke up in His glory.* I've tasted of this power first-hand and I'm gloriously tortured by this deep gut "knowing" that there is *so much more.* We are acting like we've arrived as a worship movement! But if anything, we are only sliding backwards into powerless performance.

So much still remains locked up because *we have yet to build something* worthy of His full favor, habitation and blessing— vessels solely consecrated and set apart for His glory.

FINAL THOUGHTS

The goal of worship music was never to make it as sonically competitive as possible; it was to make it as potently filled with the *intoxicating, mesmerizing and unraveling presence of Jesus as possible.* We will never lead the world by imitating the world. Our job was never to compete with the world's artistry, our job was to give the world *a taste of heaven.*

Right now, the world and the church are languishing for lack of new wine. They are longing for a taste of heaven's atmosphere and glory.

But this new wine needs a new wineskin. We need leaders who will be courageous to break with the old models and patterns and commit to building new networks, creative communities and holy coalitions. We need vintners who carry a shepherding zeal and wisdom that guards the anointing on worship leaders, communities, songs and projects; who are not only able to discern *the specific anointing and design of* God on a church or worship leader, but who are *unwilling* to release what they produce until it reflects the full measure of *both*. Leaders who are not only able to discern the visible destiny on a person, but prophetically able to call out the ones *who don't even know they're called*.

May the grace and power of God enable us to courageously birth these new vineyards and wineskins, and give us the wisdom to capture, preserve and release the new wine of heaven here on earth.

REFORMATION ITEMS

CHAPTER 9

The modern era of worship didn't come with an instruction manual.

Most of the things we have to navigate today only existed in infant form when I was growing up. Many more things like worship song royalties, public internet, social media and smart phones didn't exist at all. There were no resources or seasoned instruction for Christians, churches or spiritual leaders trying to navigate their social media platforms wisely. There's still very little. Everything we did back in the day was necessarily experimental because it was all brand new. Nobody had ever navigated these waters before. So, we let media run wild and media rapidly began to run us.

Back then we didn't know the negative impact it was going to have, but we do now. Or at least we really should. *The era of innocence has ended.* Without course correction, the same things that gave worship its global wings will become the things that undermine its mission and pervert its purpose. Lines need to be re-drawn and boundaries need to be reset.

Many of the things affecting and influencing the heart of worship these days are not things you would typically cover in a "heart of worship" talk. So, I'm going to step out of my lane for a bit because I feel strongly these things need to be addressed. We need to get very specific and practical about the external challenges we are facing as worship leaders and Levites due to media, production and industry.

Please understand I'm not trying to drag us back to the dark ages. But I am trying to get us to think about why we do what we do *in light of our mission*. My goal in specifically addressing these things is not to "lay down the law" but to provoke needed discussion and dialogue.

The bottom line is, do we want to create cultures of worship or not?

If so, we really don't need to look much farther than our own people. Do they look like they're connecting with heaven or do they look like they're connecting with a person or a stage? If the answer isn't heaven, then our job is to work to change that.

OUR FATHER'S BUSINESS

If the Father is seeking a specific kind of worshiper, then everything we do as worship communities must be brought into focus and alignment with the thing *He's seeking*. The primary question worship leaders, worship departments and worship movements should be asking themselves before making any kind of decision is: "Will this _____ help activate, grow and equip the kind of worshiper my Father is seeking?" Our use of stage production, lighting, online streaming, social media, photography, videography, etc...our worship tours, events, conferences, merchandise, books and records...*must all be run through this filter.*

We must continually ask ourselves: Are we truly attempting to awaken, activate, and equip true, spirit-filled worshipers by doing [insert cool idea]...or...are we simply attempting to build our brands and our names under the guise of a spiritual banner?

The next most important step is to be *honest* with ourselves.

The following is my personal list of reformation items. The reason they're on this list is either:

A.) I feel they lack focus and proper alignment within the church's mission as a house of prayer.

B.) I feel they are completely outside of those bounds.

Okay. Wading in...

STAGE PRODUCTION

I believe it's essential for worship communities to have a solid grid for why they do what they do when it comes to production. Most of what I've seen adopted in churches doesn't flow from any higher value system than keeping up with the church down the street, or the large global churches whose superb facilities and stages get featured in all the well-known Christian publications and become the resulting envy of all.

I get why this drives us. Nobody wants their church to feel sub-par or less-than. But I will stress this again...we get into a lot of trouble when we blindly mimic our own Christian subculture and don't carefully weigh everything against the standard of Scripture and our assigned mission.

Almost every form of stage production the church has adopted in recent years is what mainstream venues have already had in place for decades. It's clear who's leading who. The main difference is, they are houses of entertainment. We are not. Their business purpose is not our business purpose. We are houses of prayer. And this is where the lines get blurry. A lot of the stage production in entertainment venues simply helps and enhances a large crowd's ability to engage. But a lot of their stage production isn't to solely assist in engagement, *it's to entertain*. This is where our missions differ.

In worship, we are not trying to dazzle people with what's happening on stage. We are simply trying to draw a room into a unified expression of worship. We have created so many unnecessary obstacles and distractions for people who are sincerely trying to connect to God. So much of our stage production doesn't enhance unity (unless we're going for unified spectatorship) and it certainly doesn't help worship flow *vertically*. A lot of our stage production just horizontally mesmerizes people with the wrong thing.

Yes, I'm aware that heaven is going to be a dazzling, colorful, bewildering, and mesmerizing place. But there is one massive difference between heaven and earth right now, *and that's who's on the stage*. As long as it's us, that's not where we want to pull people's attention. In heaven, no one will be able to be mesmerized with anyone other than Jesus or capable of an ounce of idolatry. But on earth, that's clearly not the case.

I love that there has been a beautiful resurgence and reconnection of the arts and visuals in worship. We're beginning to see them again, *as worship*. This is so important and I'm not attacking this. But our creativity must be Spirit-led, not "cool idea" driven. I have actually encountered Spirit-led production and not only is it remarkably powerful, it doesn't distract or detract from vertical worship—it only helps it increase. But most of the production I see in houses of prayer is far more flesh than Spirit.

CHURCH AND EVENT MEDIA

I was at an event not too long ago and having a small, private prayer time with my team before leading worship that night. All of a sudden, I looked up to see someone using a mini boom to drop a camera right into the middle of our prayer huddle, and then slowly circle it around. He seemed oblivious as to why this wasn't appropriate. After trying to politely (I hope) tell him this wasn't the time or place, he respectfully retreated. It was obvious he wasn't trying to be dishonoring and I fully believe his intentions were pure. But I began to wonder how that sort of thing had even become acceptable?

I was at another event recently and the speaker brought an intense word. He talked about how the spirit of death had been attacking people in the room and then called for a response. I was shocked by the amount of people flooding the aisles and the front to receive ministry. I was called up to begin to play softly while ministry continued. Apparently, a camera guy saw this as a great chance to capture some nice, close up footage. So, while this speaker is casting out demons and delivering people and while I'm trying to stay spiritually in step with what's happening in front of me...I've got this camera guy right in my face...slowly panning his camera back and forth...back and forth. I was dumbfounded.

Dear camera and video people reading this, I don't fault you. I mean it when I say I'm deeply grateful for your service to the body of Christ. So are all the viewers who have been tremendously blessed by what you made possible for them to be a part of. This oversight is completely on us as leaders. We're the ones who should have been leading with wisdom, appropriate guidelines, and spiritual sensitivity in the area of church media. We might have understood the power and importance of media but our lack of a clear "why" and "how" left you alone to figure it out. That was irresponsible of us. I'm so sorry.

Leaders, we cannot continue to let media run without clear, God honoring guidelines. We need a wisdom for when to capture *and when not to—a greater spiritual sensitivity*. We need a reverence and a fear of the Lord to inform these choices. We need to reconsider scriptures on the importance of spiritual "hiddenness" before posting what we post. We need to take a hard look at our driving motives in all things media. The feeling of momentum operates like a drug and is causing so many people, churches and movements to stumble in its pursuit. Jesus expressly warns against practicing our righteousness before others in order to be seen by them, just as the Pharisees loved doing. I know many times I've been guilty of this.

EXCELLENCE

I believe in excellence. I believe in giving God our wholehearted best in everything we do. But I can't help feeling churches are misinterpreting and misappropriating this value to justify all kinds of misguided pursuits and purchases. For the Christian, excellence is not a value unto itself, but a value that must live continually subservient to much higher ranking values, values such as love, witness, mission, being Spirit-led, and faithfulness.

Take stage lighting for example. If the excellence of our dazzling light show does not help us produce true worshipers, then how "excellent" is it really? It may indeed be excellent, but it certainly isn't *useful* to us. It would appear it's missing the higher value it was meant to be subservient to.

Or take spontaneous, Spirit-led worship moments as another example. If we chose excellence as our highest value, *then we would never follow the Holy Spirit.* To be spontaneous—and more importantly, obedient to the prompting of the Spirit—is to risk the band screwing up because they can't follow you, or you forgetting the words to that spontaneous chorus you just started to sing. If excellence was the highest value, we would never take those risks. *But excellence isn't.* Faith and obedience *always* outrank excellence. Or more accurately, faith and obedience redefine what excellence means in our worship sets. Excellence now becomes less about a band nailing a rehearsed and curated arrangement, and more about a band playing with all their heart and skill to give wings to the unction of the Spirit.

SOCIAL MEDIA

I was a latecomer to the world of Instagram. When I finally started an account, I inaugurated it with multiple pictures of me shaving off my "No Shave November" beard in progressive redneck stages. The whole thing was a joke to me until...I decided to become a professional nature photographer. Then it got extremely serious. I kid. But only kind of. I still think I took some pretty sweet pictures.

But little did I know how much this platform would sift my soul and test my purity. I'm grateful for the true prophetic voices in my life (my wife included) who brought this lingering compromise to my attention and sent me on a year long journey of progressive disconnection to it. Just like fasting reveals the power of food over your life, so distancing yourself from social media reveals your addiction to it—all the ways it was impacting you that you couldn't see before. Social media has such a subtle way of corrupting you and steering your decisions. The larger your platform grows, the more power it has to sicken and disease your soul and shape you into a puppet and a parrot.

At present, social media is wiring our brains in the worst way. It is manipulating and compromising leaders, churches, movements and...well, most of humanity to be honest. But I'm particularly bothered by its corruption of worship. Instead of seeing holy, sacred moments in worship and responding appropriately, it's trained us to see "numbers" and "likes." Everyone's personal and intimate encounter with God has now become the new hot media commodity. When God begins to move in a gathering, instead of fully engaging with it everyone starts scrambling to get "that shot," or that sweet set of insta stories that will make everyone jealous and wish they were there.

As worship leaders and Levites, we are way more affected by this than we are letting on. It is trying and sifting our souls. It is testing our purity. And I'm here to encourage you to separate yourselves from it. Protect your heart, your purity and your spiritual authority. Create distance and put up guardrails. Block its influence on you. You will feel something beginning to reset inside you when you do.

I've had to put up guardrails on all my social media to help me focus my *desire* for significance, on what *actually* makes my life significant. I sincerely work to take my own medicine. Most days all social media apps are deleted from my devices. For every single post, I put my motives through a series of tests, always asking myself: "Why am I posting this? What is this unto? What am I seeking to accomplish? Is this what I should be posting? Am I feeding my ego in any way? Is this in accordance with the call on my life or am I just giving people what they seem to want?"

INFLUENCE

As believers, we're accountable for everything we've been given. Therefore, everything we've been given *requires stewardship*. This includes influence. But the only way to effectively steward anything is to understand *its God-intended purpose*. Do you know why you've been given influence? Have you ever asked yourself what God wants you to do with it or how He wants you to use it? Have you ever consecrated and committed your influence to His glory and not your own? The Bible is not silent on the purpose of a believer's influence, but our ignorance of it is clear. So much of what Christians do for the sake of greater influence only mimics the world and nullifies *our influence*.

So, by all means post about your dog, your cat, your house, a brilliant cup of coffee and all things great and wonderful about life. But also ask yourself, *"Am I shining the unique and specific light God has given me to shine on this earth...the one no one else can shine?"* Make sure that salt and light isn't conspicuously absent in anything you do.

THE "WORSHIP ARTIST"

A troubling trend has been growing for some time in the worship industry. We have been increasingly intermixing things that do not belong together and should have always remained separate and distinct. Worship leaders are not performing artists and nights of worship are not concerts. And yet, in this regard, we continue to intentionally and unintentionally marry what is sacred with what is common. This should not be. Worship is holy. Worship is unto God. Worship is for His pleasure and His pleasure alone. It cannot coincide with a night of entertainment on behalf of people. That is an unholy coalition, as is marrying a worship leader with our definition of a performing artist.

If you are going to engage in leading the body and bride of Christ into worship and adoration, you are not a performer, *you are a priest*. As worship leaders, we are entrusted with two of the most sacred things to the heart of God: *His glory and His bride*. To forget His burning zeal over either of these two things and become complacent, irreverent and irresponsible, is to risk great judgment. Our priestly assignment is far more glorious, sobering and weighty than that of any performing artist and we cannot afford to confuse the two.

WORSHIP EVENTS AND TICKET SALES

I have been an itinerant worship leader for the past fifteen years. I'm no stranger to the logistics of worship events and have done many ticketed nights of worship. I understand all the reasons we choose to ticket nights of worship, but I've never been able to quiet my spirit on this. Something about charging someone to come to a night of worship just feels like a holy violation to me.

I know the risks of doing it the other ways, but I will gladly take those risks. I'm not saying there won't be exceptions, but for the most part, I would rather be hurt financially or simply not travel, than continue to violate this.

I don't think this is necessarily a conviction everyone must carry, but I do believe everyone who does events should wrestle through this. I am fully aware that many people are able to buy tickets for nights of worship in total purity and worship God without hindrance. But I have seen firsthand that ticket sales inevitably create a consumer mentality and a performance expectation that wars against a heavenly focused night of pure, undistracted devotion. The hint of a consumer mentality will immediately sicken the heart of devotion.

The higher the ticket prices become, the weirder this thing gets. And the term "weird" fails to do justice to the new practice of offering preferred seating and backstage access at a premium price. How is this not the very thing Jesus so violently rebuked when He said, *"Do not make my Father's house a house of trade"*? I'm having a hard time making a distinction.

Let me be clear: I do see the tremendous value of inviting a leader or a ministry to come and make a spiritual deposit into your church or region. I've seen the fruit of this time and time again. However, I still hate using ticket sales as the primary means to finance this. I feel quite strongly that there is a better, more kingdom way. A way that helps us preserve the purity of worship and the sacredness of the worship assembly. If you believe in something happening in your city in the realm of worship, there are other creative ways to finance this besides selling tickets.

WORSHIP SONGWRITING

Worship songs can generate a tremendous amount of royalties. Most churches pay a small licensing fee for the songs they lead during their Sunday services. These fees are then distributed to the writers of those worship songs as royalties. The more churches lead a worship song, the more royalties flow. I would love to say that all publishing companies, record labels, worship leaders and worship song writers are oblivious to this and have remained completely pure in their motives. But... I really can't.

The only thing I can say with confidence is that a "lab room" of professional writers all trying to crack the corporate code and attempting to write worship songs the masses will sing... *is not pleasing to the Lord*. The same would go for anyone, in any situation or context, who is writing a worship song with a hint of that motive in their heart.

The many songs being written this way are not filling the church with the beauty and fragrance of true worship but rather the loveless clamor of profit-seeking choruses.

CLOSING

Again, I want to create dialogue, not dogma. I realize many of the items I address in this chapter are not black and white and there is plenty of room for differing opinions. Regardless, much of what is rapidly unfolding in the area of worship today *must be challenged* because it is not only out of alignment with our mission, it is *sabotaging it*. We must look at every area of worship we've been given oversight of and fearlessly call to account anything perverting our purpose or keeping us from faithful, Biblical execution of our mission as worshiping communities. We are not victims *or* innocent bystanders of our media or production departments, event managers, or industry leaders. Let's put away passivity and complacency and lead with conviction in this moment.

THE FUTURE
CHAPTER 10

While I was writing this book, I was challenged by a friend to pray into a prophetic forecast concerning the future of worship. As I prayed into this, I believe the Lord brought several thoughts to mind. To call these thoughts "prophetic" seems a bit strong, so I'll simply share them as a personal sense of what I feel the Lord leading us into. I believe there is a purifying alliance waiting to be made that will result in the worship movement being strengthened and propelled into a new season of fiery anointing and fresh creativity.

Here is what I desire to see: I desire to see the worship movement marry the prayer movement and the mission's movement. I firmly believe that if worship is re-anchored in ministry to the Lord and ministry to the world, it will explode with fresh life, creativity and power.

A NEW ALLIANCE

The worship movement has never thrived in isolation. The more isolated it gets, the more visionless and unfocused it becomes. Left to its own devices the worship movement just serves itself. It writes songs for itself and awards itself. In order to get back to a place of health and vitality, the worship movement will need to break with old, destructive alliances and form new, healthy ones. The alliance that is killing the worship movement at present, is its alliance to industry. Simply put, we are at our worst when we allow this partnership to have any kind of domineering influence over us. We need to break with this corrupting alliance, cut off its influence, and re-give ourselves to the work of mission and prayer.

Ministry to the Lord and ministry to the poor will purify the worship movement in a stunning way if we allow it. If we would fully and willingly give ourselves to the ministry of intercession and the proclamation of the gospel, *oh what a fire would begin to be released in our hearts!* If we would only come out from under the stronghold of small, mission-less, prayer-less, godless, profit-driven thinking and begin to labor and burn to see the kingdom of heaven released on earth, *oh what songs of power, depth and devotion would explode from our souls!*

It is my firm conviction that songs carrying wrecking encounters with Jesus can only be born in a specific environment. We're trying to birth them in our isolated, insulated, musical, and theoretical songwriting "lab" rooms. But songs of encounter are not born there. They are born as we touch heaven's glory in our prayer rooms and prayer closets and as we engage in real-time ministry with the brokenness of the world through mission.

A NEW AND ANCIENT WAY

I see a new expression of an ancient kind of worship leader emerging, leaders whose lives of devotion are once again rooted in the rhythms of prayer and the mission of Jesus. Any leader who will anchor themselves in ministry to the Lord and ministry to the lost and the least will be gloriously immune to everything seeking to sabotage the purity and power of worship in this moment. You simply can't minister to the Lord in frequent prayer and consistent outreach to others and stay entitled, spiritually lazy, prideful, or self-indulgent.

I believe that if any worship leader or worshiper desires to see the full anointing on their life come forth, they will join themselves to the mission of Jesus who is both Intercessor and Reconciler.

The days of professional career driven worship leading, and songwriting may bo rapidly dwindling. This does not sadden me in the least. *It means that groat purity is about to burst onto the scene.* Worship songs and worship leaders will once again be birthed in the most unusual places. Songs written by people in the marketplace, the factories, and the fields will start to flow again. Songs of heartfelt simplicity, written by the "common" man or woman, will spring up once more. We have been *greatly* missing these songs.

WORSHIP AND PRAYER

Every time I hear someone who is full of the knowledge of the Lord and walking in a royal, priestly authority in prayer, I'm reminded of the kind of leader the worship movement is missing. *We are missing worship leaders who have completely given themselves to the ministry of prayer and are drenched in intimacy and deep communion with God.* But these kinds of worship leaders will never be formed through a typical Sunday service rotation where they only get to lead twice a month. These kinds of leaders must be formed in the daily discipline of prayer and focused ministry to the Lord.

We desperately need greenhouses of prayer where worship leaders can be spiritually trained and developed without being crippled by the pressure of a Sunday service. Over the years, I have observed that every worship leader who carried a real sense of intimacy and connection with the Lord, who could flow in the spontaneous or the prophetic, and was able to break through in dry and difficult sets, *almost always* had some kind of history with the prayer movement. I could say the exact same thing about musicians.

So, if there is one thing I have determined in my heart, it's that any worship community I build from here on out is going to be a community *built on prayer*. I'm convinced this is the only way to raise up leaders and musicians who will carry the anointing, the skill set, the power and the intimacy with God needed for real spiritual breakthrough.

If we want leaders who are marked by glory, *they must encounter glory*. Moreover, they must learn how to consistently chart a path to its dwelling place—a well-worn highway in their heart that takes them there every time. This is what ministry to the Lord is all about. *This is what prayer is all about.* Every time we give ourselves to the ministry of prayer, we are creating internal highways that lead us into heavenly realms of glory and deep intimacy with Jesus. This is where we truly discover our spiritual identity and authority—*it's in the presence of His Majesty.*

I could write so much on prayer here, but instead I will simply encourage you to go after the many resources available on this topic. Even more so, I want to encourage you to determine in your heart to become a person marked by prayer. *It is the mark of intimacy.* Give yourself to a concentrated season of prayer and lay this foundation in your life.

WORSHIP AND THE HARVEST

There has always been a profound connection between worship and the harvest. Just recently I was watching a documentary on a small band of missionaries in the Middle East. As I watched, it was almost as if I could feel songs of great potency and power waiting to be unearthed in the soil of great surrender and sacrifice—waiting to be written through lives laid down and given over to the proclamation of the gospel.

Worship flows into mission. It is in fact, *the mission.* Another way of understanding the great commission is to see it as a call to "to go and make worshipers." Worshipers are the fruit of discipleship. Worshipers are the thing the Father is seeking. *The worship movement should be the one driving the mission's movement.* We must yet again become the movement that will go into all the earth and preach the gospel of Jesus Christ—a movement of people who go into the market squares, the lost regions, and the realms of deep darkness with the torch of our testimony of Jesus and the power of His blood.

No missionary on the front lines needs to fight for their purity the way leaders on big stages and tour buses do. When you worship from a place where you know your life is on the line, you tend to be pretty focused on what matters. I believe we could be stepping into a season of greater persecution as a church and worshiping community. We must re-align ourselves now in preparation. We must burn like we've never burned before for the glory of God and risk like we've never risked before. It will be those on the front lines who will carry this forward.

The future is in the field—it is in the streets and the marketplaces. The future is in the "underground" gatherings of undivided hearts lifting holy, faith-filled prayers of adoration and declaration. The future is praying, missional, worshiping communities who will give fresh creative expression to the heart of God for the world and the heart of the church for God. They will be small and intimate, but their impact will be deep and wide. They will be far more creative, effective and innovative than we ever could imagine.

RETURNING
CHAPTER 11

I'm convinced there's a generation waiting to catch fire. Even now, they are cultivating and stoking the internal flame of love, passion and pure fervency for Jesus. He *will be* their one true desire and the sound of their lives will cry, *"All is for Your glory!"* They are an army of hidden ones whose righteousness will soon break forth like the dawn. I'm convinced there are mothers and fathers of worship who have allowed their voices to be silenced, quieted and tamed, but that is ending—the Lord is restoring your spiritual authority in this hour. I also feel the Lord is calling those whose flame "once burned bright and clear"[8] but the pain of life, disappointment, personal failure and misunderstanding have taken the wind out of your sails and led you into resignation. The Lord is awakening an old flame, and He will cause it to burn brighter in your latter years than it ever did in the zeal of your youth.

We stand in a moment of purification. I'm writing this book in the midst of a global pandemic that has shut down church services, programs, conferences and Christian events of almost every kind. This is a moment of *reset*. The money that once flowed through the industries and enterprises we built around worship is drying up. Tour buses and venues stand empty. I can't think of a better time than now to let go of old structures, wine skins, vices, entangling sins, pride, ego, platform, and anything and everything that has been grieving the heart of God.

In this shaking, we are being given a precious opportunity to repent and return to the Lord. To take back up the mantle of purity, and in returning and rest, discover the new things God desires to do in us and through us.

But the great and glorious prize for our repentance will not be the "new" thing, or the "new" sound, or a re-packaged, re-branded spin off of the old thing.

It will be Jesus Himself. He will be our *great* and *glorious* portion and prize. He is the drink our parched souls have been thirsting after.

If we get Him, we get *everything. He is everything.*

Over the last twenty years, I feel like I've been a part of every kind of Christian event you can possibly imagine: from charities, to small groups, to Sunday mornings, to Christian conferences, to Christian festivals, to youth camps, to global worship tours, to radio events, and even the hotly pursued and highly elusive dream of leading a "stadium" in worship. I've written hit songs, made records, and received accolades and awards. I've been a part of the "buzz" that follows the "new thing" and experienced the heat and craze of momentum. I've known varying degrees of platform, influence and acclaim. By all accounts, *I have lived the worship leader "dream."*

So, hear me as I write this with an intensity and emotion more akin to anguish than a sense of accomplishment: *It all means NOTHING without Him.*

None of it is precious to me. *I would trade it all for just one more moment with Him. To be a doorkeeper in any house where His presence dwells.*

So many are chasing the wrong dream and the empty thing. Forgive me an Ecclesiastical moment while I cry out, *"Vanity of vanities. All is vanity!"* My friends, the dream is *nothing...worse than nothing...without* Him. Better is one day in His presence than a lifetime of fulfilled dreams without Him. HE...is the dream. Faithfulness to *Jesus* is the dream! The only dream worth living for!

We are living in an apocalyptic time. But whether Jesus returns in our lifetime or whether He waits another thousand years makes no difference. Because one way or another, at the end of our lives, we will meet Him and stand face to face! The only thing that will matter then will be a life of *wholehearted devotion to Him.* Plans, career, platform, numbers, provision, hits, notoriety...what will they profit? What will they gain? If those deeds weren't done out of wholehearted surrender, love and obedience...they will gain *nothing! Absolutely nothing.* Consumed in a flash of fire.

If there was ever a moment to abandon anything that distracts, entangles, or connects you to compromise, *this would be that moment.* I would rather take the lowliest, service-based position in society than be a career driven worship leader on the day of His coming. I want to be pure, fiery, without compromise and joyfully engaged in the assignments He's given me when that trumpet sounds and the sky is rolled back like a scroll.

This book is my plea and I'm writing it with all of my heart. This is my attempt to be a faithful voice in this hour. I confess at times I've wondered if it has come too late. But I also believe every day we're given on this earth can be a day of redemption. As the criminal crucified on the cross next to Jesus proves, no day of redemption is without its fruit. Even *one hour* of wholehearted returning to the Lord can make all the difference, *for all eternity*.

At this moment, God is purifying the sons of Levi:

> *For he is like refiner's fire and like fuller's soap. He will sit as a refiner and purifier of silver, and he will purify the sons of Levi and refine them like gold and silver, and they will bring offerings in righteousness to the Lord.*
> Malachi 3:2-3

So, come! Let us return unto the LORD! Let us rend our hearts and not our garments! Let us consecrate and declare a solemn assembly! A marked moment of departure from all that has corrupted us and *equally*...a marked moment of fresh consecration and wholehearted surrender. From this day forward, let us be ministers to Him who only burn with *"love incorruptible."*

The world is hungry to worship.

They are longing to know and glorify Jesus.

They are simply waiting for us to cast off all hindrances, weights, sins, and religious excess, *fix our eyes on Jesus,* and worship Him so radically, extravagantly, profusely and gloriously, we imperil our very lives.

This is the point of life itself. Let pure, true, Spirit-filled, wholehearted worshipers, *rise.*

NOTES

Introduction

[1] Matt Redman, "The Heart of Worship," The Heart of Worship, 1999. Thankyou Music (PRS) (CapitolCMGPublishing.com) CCLI#: 2296522

Chapter 1

[2] A. W. Tozer in The Best of A. W. Tozer, as quoted in Making New Discoveries (Anaheim, CA.: Insight for Living, 1996), 29. See also A. W. Tozer; Worship: The Missing Jewel of the Evangelical Church (1971).

Chapter 4

[3] C.S Lewis, Mere Christianity (first published in Great Britain by Geoffrey Bles 1952, © C.S. Lewis Pre Ltd 1942).

[4] Dietrich Bonhoeffer, The Cost of Discipleship (New York, NY: SCM Press Ltd. 1959, Touchstone,1995), 89.

[5] Basilea Schlink, My All for Him (Darmstadt, Germany: Evangelical Sisterhood of Mary, original in German 1969, translated into English 2017), 21.

Chapter 7

[6] J. I. Packer, Concise Theology: A Guide to Historic Christian Beliefs (Carol Stream, IL: Foundation for Reformation, Tyndale, 1993), xii.

[7] Belinda Huang, "What Kind of Impact does our Music Really Make on Society?" Sonicbids accessed 12/1/2020 at https://blog.sonicbids.com/what-kind-of-impact-does-our-music-really-make-on-society

Chapter11

[8] Keith Green, "Oh Lord, You're Beautiful," So You Want to Go Back to Egypt, 1980. Copyright Capitol CMG Genesis, Birdwing Music and Capitol CMG Genesis, Universal Music: Brentwood Benson Publishing CCLI#:14514

ABOUT THE AUTHOR

Jeremy Riddle is a pastor, worship leader and songwriter. He carries a deep passion for God's glory and His church. His heart burns to see purity restored. Originally from New Jersey, Jeremy was first introduced to contemporary worship as a twelve-year-old boy through YWAM (Youth With A Mission).

Not long after, Jeremy and his family transitioned to Southern California and began attending the Vineyard Anaheim where he continued to grow as a worship leader and songwriter. At the age of twenty-three, Jeremy accepted his first full-time ministry position at Anaheim as a Junior High Pastor. It was during his six years in this role that his passion for the church and his call to disciple worship leaders solidified and deepened.

In 2009, Jeremy and his family moved to Redding, California, where they attended Bethel Church and were a part of the Bethel Music Collective. After nearly a decade, the Riddles felt God lead them to move back to Southern California. Without it being the original plan, they ended up back on staff with Vineyard Anaheim. They currently serve as the Worship, Prayer and Creativity Pastors where they are partnering to re-birth a regional and global worship and prayer movement focused on wholehearted devotion to the Lord.

Jeremy and his wife Katie have five amazing children who they consider to be their greatest ministry assignment and legacy.

Learn more about Jeremy at **JeremyRiddle.com**.

Made in the USA
Monee, IL
24 January 2023